NEW SELECTED POEMS

ALSO BY DANNIE ABSE

Poetry

After Every Green Thing
Walking Under Water
Tenants of the House
Poems, Golders Green
A Small Desperation
Funland and Other Poems
Collected Poems 1948–1976
Way Out in the Centre
Ask the Bloody Horse
White Coat, Purple Coat: Poems 1948–1988
Remembrance of Crimes Past
On the Evening Road
Arcadia, One Mile
New and Collected Poems
Running Late

Editor

The Hutchinson Book of Post-war British Poets
Twentieth Century Anglo-Welsh Poetry
Voices in the Gallery (with Joan Abse)
The Music Lover's Literary Companion (with Joan Abse)

Plays

The View from Row G: Three plays

Novels

Ash on a Young Man's Sleeve
Some Corner of an English Field
O. Jones, O. Jones
There Was A Young Man from Cardiff
The Strange Case of Dr Simmonds and Dr Glas

Other Prose

Medicine on Trial
A Poet in the Family
A Strong Dose of Myself (Confessions Stories, Essays)
Journals from the Ant Heap
Intermittent Journals
Goodbye, Twentieth Century
The Two Roads Taken
The Presence

NEW SELECTED POEMS

Dannie Abse

HUTCHINSON
LONDON

Published by Hutchinson 2009

2 4 6 8 10 9 7 5 3 1

First published in Great Britain in 2009 by
Hutchinson
Random House, 20 Vauxhall Bridge Road,
London SW1V 2SA

www.rbooks.co.uk

Addresses for companies within The Random House Group Limited can be found at:
www.randomhouse.co.uk/offices.htm

The Random House Group Limited Reg. No. 954009

A CIP catalogue record for this book
is available from the British Library

ISBN 9780091931155

The Random House Group Limited supports The Forest Stewardship Council (FSC), the leading international forest certification organisation. All our titles that are printed on Greenpeace approved FSC certified paper carry the FSC logo. Our paper procurement policy can be found at www.rbooks.co.uk/environment

Mixed Sources
Product group from well-managed forests and other controlled sources
www.fsc.org Cert no. TT-COC-2139
© 1996 Forest Stewardship Council

Typeset by Palimpsest Book Production Limited,
Grangemouth, Stirlingshire
Printed and bound in Great Britain by
Clays Ltd, St Ives plc

Contents

Part One: Earlier Poems

Part Two: Poems 1967–1989

Part Four: Longer Poems

Foreword

Poets tend to have shorter writing careers than novelists. The intense vision of poets who die young remains strong, whereas those who write throughout a long life may lose touch with their original genius and find that their poems turn prosaic: the later Wordsworth for example. But Dannie Abse runs triumphantly counter to this tendency, and this is why the publication of his *New Selected Poems* is such a joyful and important event.

Just over sixty years ago, Hutchinson published Dannie Abse's first collection, *After Every Green Thing*, and in 2009 the same publisher has produced this volume, which contains Abse's own selection of his work from six decades as well as some new poems and reworkings of others. Such poetic longevity is remarkable, as is the fact that he has remained with this one publisher for all his original poetry and much of his prose. But even more impressive is the continuity and deepening of his vision.

Dannie Abse's early poems were steeped in the romantic lyricism of the 1940s and were influenced especially by Dylan Thomas. As his work grew, it became simpler and less rhetorical, but more profound – so that anyone who now encounters one of his poems can immediately grasp its meaning and enjoy its musicality, but then realize that this is only the beginning and that there are other, sometimes less comfortable, levels to explore.

His themes and subject-matter have always ranged widely, from the playful and the implacably domestic, through parables and mythologies (both Welsh and Jewish) to the horrors of recent history and of the human psyche (the latter often seen from the privileged and lonely perspective of the doctor). But while his gaze remains clear-eyed his tone is always humane, full of understanding and affirmation. His work covers a variety of writing disciplines – fiction, memoir, criticism, medicine – but poetry is its heartland. His most recent poems, written after the death of his wife Joan in a car-crash, are a revelation. He remains, as Elaine Feinstein has said, one of our few great poets of married love.

I have been Dannie Abse's editor at Hutchinson since the early 1970s. Our first editorial dealings were transatlantic, when he was Writer in Residence at Princeton University and his volume of autobiography, *A Poet in the Family*, was being prepared. But since then, through friendship and the publication of seventeen books, I have come to realize the close identity of the man and his work and the great quality of both.

Anthony Whittome,
Hutchinson, 2009

I

Earlier Poems

The Uninvited

They came into our lives unasked for.
There was light momentarily, a flicker of wings,
a dance, a voice, and then they went out
again, like a light, leaving us not so much
in darkness, but in a different place
and alone as never before.

So we have been changed
and our vision no longer what it was,
and our hopes no longer what they were;
so a piece of us has gone out with them also,
a cold dream subtracted without malice,

the weight of another world added also,
and we did not ask, we did not ask ever
for those who stood smiling
and with flowers before the open door.

We did not beckon them in, they came in uninvited,
the sunset pouring from their shoulders,
so they walked through us as they would through water,
and we are here, in a different place,
changed and incredibly alone,
and we did not know, we do not know ever.

Letter to *The Times*

Sir, I have various complaints to make.
The roses, first. When they are ripped
from the earth expiring, we sigh for them,
prescribe tap-water, aspirin, and salt.
But when we lie down under the same earth,
in a dry silly box, do they revive us?
Their odour of rose-ghosts does not change
at all, and they continue to call out
in their red and white morse the old, old
messages as if nothing had happened. Again,
consider trees. My God, the impresario
trees. Just try, Sir, just try to cut one down
in Fitzjohn's Avenue at three o'clock
in the ordinary afternoon. You will be
prosecuted. Soon the Householders will arrange
themselves into a deranged *mob*. They'll grow
Hitler moustaches, Mussolini chins. Frightful,
and write oathy letters to the Council,
naming you *tree-criminal*. Yet tell me, when
the bombs met their shadows in London,
amidst the ruins of voices, did one tree, just one
tree write an angry note in its sly green ink?
No, they only dropped faded tears in autumn
selfishly thinking of their own hamadryads . . .
BUSINESS AS USUAL was, and is, their trite
slogan. Away then with trees and roses.
They are inhuman. Away also with rivers:
the disgusting Ganges bleeding from Brahma's
big toe; the Rubicon cause of a Civil War;
the Acheron, River of Sorrows; Tiber that drowned
Horatius the One-Eyed; the sweating Rhône,

Rhine, Don, and the vulgar Volga, not to
mention the garrulous Mississippi with its
blatant river-smell. Even the English
rivers can do no more than reflect inverted
values, turn chaste swans upside down
like so many flies on the roof of the waters.
Swans, however, *cannot* swim upside down.
At least, I have never seen them. Is this distortion
of truth deliberate? Has ever one river,
one river, Sir, written eulogies of waterfalls
to plead for the reprieve of Mankind? And stars,
so indifferent and delinquent, stars which we have
decorated with glittering adjectives more numerous
than those bestowed on Helen's eyes – do they
warn us when they fall? Not a hint.
Not a star-wink. They are even too lazy
to shine when we are most awake. Creatures
of night, they are probably up to immoral
purposes. You can't trust a star, that's sure.
So when the greenfly is in the rose,
and the dragonfly drops its shadow in the river;
when the axe hides in the tree with its listening
shriek, and clouds gag the starlight
with grey handkerchiefs – I contend, Sir,
that we should pity them no more,
but concern ourselves with more natural things.

1949

Duality

Twice upon a time,
there was a man who had two faces,
two faces but one profile:
not Jekyll and Hyde, not good and bad,
and if one were cut, the other would bleed –
two faces different as hot and cold.

At night, hung on the hooks on the wall
above that man's minatory head,
one wants brass where one wants gold,
one sees white and one sees black,
and one mouth eats the other
until the second sweet mouth bites back.

They dream their separate dreams
hanging on the wall above the bed.
The first voice cries: 'He's not what he seems,'
but the second one sighs: 'He is what he is,'
then one shouts 'wine' and the other screams 'bread',
and so they will all his raving days
until they die on his double-crossed head.

At signposts he must wear them both.
Each would go their separate ways
as the East or the West wind blows –
and dark and light they both would praise,
but one would melt, the other one freeze.

I am that man twice upon this time:
my two voices sing to make one rhyme.
Death I love and Death I hate,

(I'll be with you soon and late).
Love I love and Love I loathe
God I mock and God I prove,
yes, myself I kill, myself I save.

Now, now, I hang these masks on the wall.
Oh Time, take one and leave me all
lest four tears from two eyes fall.

The Trial

The heads around the table disagree,
some say hang him from the gallows tree.

Some say high and some say low
to swing, swing, swing, when the free winds blow.

I wanted to be myself, no more,
so I screwed off the face that I always wore,

I pulled out the nails one by one –
I'd have given that face to anyone.

For those vile features were hardly mine;
to wear another's face is a spiritual crime.

Why, imagine the night when I would wed
to kiss with wrong lips in the bridal bed . . .

But now the crowd screams loud in mockery:
Oh string him up from the gallows tree.

Silence! the Judge commands, or I'll clear the court,
to hang a man up is not a sport –

though some say high and some say low
to swing, swing, swing, when the free winds blow.

Prisoner, allow me once more to ask:
what did you do with your own pure mask?

I told you, your honour, I threw it away,
it was only made of skin-coloured clay.

A face is a man, a bald juryman cries,
for one face lost, another man dies.

Gentlemen, this citizen we daren't acquit
until we know what he did with it.

It was only a face, your honour, that I lost;
how much can such a sad thing cost?

A mask is a lifetime, my bad man,
to replace such a gift nobody can.

Consider the case of that jovial swan
who took a god's face off to put a bird's face on

and Leda swooning by the side of the sea
and the swan's eyes closed in lechery.

No! No! your honour, my aim was just –
I did what every true man must.

Quiet, prisoner! Why I remember a priest remark
that he picked up a dog's face in the dark,

then he got as drunk as a man can be
and barked at God in blasphemy.

But it was a human face, sir, I cast away;
for that offence do I have to pay?

The heads around the table disagree,
some say hang him from the gallows tree.

Some say high and some say low
to swing, swing, swing, when the free winds blow.

At the back of the courtroom quietly stand
his father and mother hand-in-hand.

They can't understand the point of this case
or why he discarded his own dear face.

But it's not *my* face, father, he had said,
I don't want to die in a strange, wrong bed.

Look in the mirror, mother, stare in deep;
is that mask your own, yours to keep?

The mirror is oblong, the clock is round,
all our wax faces go underground.

Once, I built a bridge right into myself
to ransack my soul for invisible wealth

and, afterwards, I tore off my mask because
I found not the person I thought I was.

With the wrong mask, another man's life I live –
I must seek my own face, find my own grave.

The heads around the table disagree,
some say hang him from the gallows tree.

Some say high and some say low
to swing, swing, swing, when the free winds blow.

I'll sum up, the severe Judge moans,
showing the white of his knucklebones.

What is a face but the thing that you see,
the symbol and fate of identity?

How would we recognize each from each:
a dog from a man – which face on a leash?

And when tears fall where no face is,
will the tears be mine or will they be his?

To select hot coal or gold no man is free,
each choice being determined by identity.

But exchange your face then what you choose
is gained, like love, by what you lose.

Now you twelve jurymen please retire,
put your right hands in ice and your left in fire.

A hole where the face was frightens us,
and a man who can choose is dangerous.

So what is your verdict going to be,
should he be hung from a gallows tree?

Oh some say high and some say low
to swing, swing, swing, when the free winds blow.

Soho: Saturday Night

Always Cain, anonymous amidst the poor,
Abel dead in his eye, and over his damned sore
a khaki muffler, loiters, a fugitive in Soho,
enters The Golden Calf Club and hears Esau,

dishevelled and drunk, cursing kith and kin.
'A mess of pottage!' Esau strokes an unshaven chin
and strikes a marble table-top. Then hairy hands
fidget dolefully, raise up a glass of gin.

Outside, Joseph, dyspnoeic, regards a star
convexing over Dean Street, coughs up a flower
from ruined lungs – rosy petals on his tongue –
recalls the Pit and wounds of many a colour.

Traffic lights change. With tapping white stick
a giant crosses the road between the frantic
taxis. A philistine pimp laughs. Dancing
in The Nude Show Delilah suddenly feels sick.

Ruth, too, the innocent, was gullibly led,
lay down half-clothed on a brassy railing bed
of Mr Boaz of Bayswater. Now, too late, weeps
antiseptic tears, wishes she were dead.

Who goes home? Nebuchadnezzar to the doss-
house where, all night, he'll turn and toss.
Lunchtime, in Soho Square, he munched the grass
and now he howls at strangers as they pass.

In Café Babylon, Daniel, interpreter of dreams,
listens to Belshazzar, a shy lad in his teens:
'A soiled finger moved across the lavatory wall.'
Growing up is not so easy as it seems.

Prophets, like tipsters, awaiting the Advent.
Beggar Job, under the flashing advertisement
for toothpaste, the spirochaete in his brain,
groans. Chalks a lurid picture on the pavement.

The Golden Calf closes. Who goes home? All
tourists to Nod; psalmists from their pub crawl;
they leave unshaved Soho to its dawn furnace
of affliction, its wormwood and its gall.

1948, 1995

Letter to Alex Comfort

Alex, perhaps a colour of which neither of us had dreamt
may appear in the test-tube with God knows what admonition.
Ehrlich, certainly, was one who broke down the mental doors,
yet only after his six hundred and sixth attempt.

Koch also, painfully, and with true German thoroughness,
eliminated the impossible to prove that too many of us

are dying from the same disease. Visible, on the slide
at last – Death – and the thin bacilli of an ancient distress.

Still I, myself, don't like Germans, but prefer the unkempt
voyagers who, like butterflies drunk with suns,
can only totter crookedly in the dazed air
to reach, charmingly, their destination as if by accident.

That Greek one, then, is my hero who watched the bath water
rise above his navel, and rushed out naked, 'I found it,
I found it' into the street in all his shining and forgot
that others would only stare at his genitals.
    What laughter!

Or Newton, leaning in Woolsthorpe against the garden wall,
forgot his indigestion and all such trivialities,
but gaped up at heaven in just surprise, and, with
true gravity, witnessed the vertical apple fall.

O what a marvellous observation! Who would have reckoned
that such a pedestrian miracle could alter history,
that, henceforward, everyone must fall, whatever
their rank, at thirty-two feet per second, per second?

You too, I know, have waited for doors to fly open, played
with your cold chemicals, written long letters
to the Press; listened to the truth afraid, and dug deep
into the wriggling earth for a rainbow with an honest spade.

But nothing rises. Neither spectres, nor oil, nor love.
And the old professor must think you mad, Alex, as you
    rehearse

poems in the laboratory like vows, and curse those clever
  scientists
who dissect away the wings and haggard heart from the dove.

Epithalamion

Singing, today I married my white girl
beautiful in a barley field.
Green on thy finger a grass blade curled,
so with this ring I thee wed, I thee wed,
and send our love to the loveless world
of all the living and all the dead.

Now, no more than vulnerable human,
we, more than one, less than two,
are nearly ourselves in a barley field –
and only love is the rent that's due
though the bailiffs of time return anew
to all the living but not the dead.

Shipwrecked, the sun sinks down harbours
of a sky, unloads its liquid cargoes
of marigolds, and I and my white girl
lie still in the barley – who else wishes
to speak, what more can be said
by all the living against all the dead?

Come then all you wedding guests:
green ghost of trees, gold of barley,
you blackbird priests in the field,
you wind that shakes the pansy head
fluttering on a stalk like a butterfly;
come the living and come the dead.

Listen flowers, birds, winds, worlds,
tell all today that I married
more than a white girl in the barley –
for today I took to my human bed
flower and bird and wind and world,
and all the living and all the dead.

Elegy for Dylan Thomas

All down the valleys they are talking,
and in the community of the smoke-laden town.
Tomorrow, through bird trailed skies, across labouring
waves,
wrong-again Emily will come to the dandelion yard
and, with rum tourists, inspect his grave.

Death was his voluntary marriage,
and his poor silence sold to that rich and famous bride.
Beleaguered in that essential kiss he rode

the whiskey-meadows of her breath till, mortal,
voicless,
he gave up his nailed ghost and he died.

No more to celebrate
his disinherited innocence or your half-buried heart
drunk as a butterfly, or sober as black.
Now, one second from earth, not even for the sake
of love can his true energy come back.

So cease your talking.
Too familiar you blaspheme his name and collected
legends:
some tears fall soundlessly and aren't the same
as those that drop with obituary explosions.
Suddenly, others who sing seem older and lame.

But far from the blind country of prose,
wherever his burst voice goes about you or through
you,
look up in surprise, in a hurt public house
or in a rain-blown street, and see how
no fat ghost but a quotation cries.

Stranger, he is laid to rest
not in the nightingale dark nor in the canary light.
At the dear last, the yolk broke in his head,
blood of his soul's egg in a splash of bright
voices and now he is dead.

December, 1953

Anniversary

(At Primrose Hill, London)

The tree grows down from a bird.
The strong grass pulls up the earth
to a hill. Wade here, my dear,
through green shallows of daisies.
I hear the voice talking that is dead
behind the voice that is talking now.
The clocks of the smoky town
strike a quiet, grating sound.
Tomorrow will be the same.
Two sit on this hill and count
two moving from the two that stayed.

What happens to a flame blown out?
What perishes? Not this view,
nor my magnified hand in yours
whatever hurt and angers done.
I breathe in air the dead breathed out.
When first you inclined your face
to mine, my sweet ally came,
with your brown eyes purely wide.
My right hand on your left breast
I said, I have little to tell my dear.
For the pure bird, a pure cage.

Oh the silence that you lost
blind in the pandemonium
of the kiss and ruined was.
My dear, my dear, what perishes?
I hear this voice in a voice to come.

The Game

Follow the crowds to where the turnstiles click.
The terraces fill. *Hoompa*, blares the brassy band.
Saturday afternoon has come to Ninian Park
and, beyond the goal posts, in the Canton Stand
between black spaces, a hundred matches spark.

Waiting, we recall records, legendary scores:
Fred Keenor, Hardy, in a royal blue shirt.
The very names, sad as the old songs, open doors
before our time where someone else was hurt.
Now, like an injured beast, the great crowd roars.

The coin is spun. Here all is simplified,
and we are partisan who cheer the Good,
hiss at passing Evil. Was Lucifer offside?
A wing falls down when cherubs howl for blood.
Demons have agents: the Referee is bribed.

The white ball smacked the crossbar. Satan rose
higher than the others in the smoked brown gloom
to sink on grass in a ballet dancer's pose.
Again, it seems, we hear a familiar tune
not quite identifiable. A distant whistle blows.

Memory of faded games, the discarded years;
talk of Aston Villa, Orient, and the Swans.
Half-time, the band played the same military airs
as when the Bluebirds once were champions.
Round touchlines the same cripples in their chairs.

Mephistopheles had his joke. The honest team
dribbles ineffectively, no one can be blamed.
Infernal backs tackle, inside forwards scheme,
and if they foul us need we be ashamed?
Heads up! Oh for a Ted Drake, a Dixie Dean.

'Saved' or else, discontents, we are transferred
long decades back, like Faust must pay that fee.
The Night is early. Great phantoms in us stir
as coloured jerseys hover, move diagonally
on the damp turf, and our eidetic visions blur.

God sign our souls! Because the obscure staff
of Hell rule this world, jugular fans guessed
the result halfway through the second half,
and those who know the score just seem depressed.
Small boys swarm the field for an autograph.

Silent the stadium. The crowds have all filed out.
Only the pigeons beneath the roofs remain.
The clean programmes are trampled underfoot,
and natural the dark, appropriate the rain,
while, under lamp-posts, threatening newsboys shout.

Return to Cardiff

'Hometown'; well, most admit an affection for a city:
grey, tangled streets I cycled on to school, my first cigarette
in the back lane, and, fool, my first botched love affair.
First everything. Faded torments; self-indulgent pity.

The journey to Cardiff seemed less a return than a raid
on mislaid identities. Of course the whole locus smaller:
the mile-wide Taff now a stream, the castle not as in some
  black,
gothic dream, but a decent sprawl, a joker's toy façade.

Unfocused voices in the wind, associations, clues,
odds and ends, fringes caught, as when, after the doctor quit,
a door opened and I glimpsed the white, enormous face
of my grandfather, suddenly aghast with certain news.

Unable to define anything I can hardly speak,
and still I love the place for what I wanted it to be
as much as for what it unashamedly is
now for me, a city of strangers, alien and bleak.

Unable to communicate I'm easily betrayed,
uneasily diverted by mere sense reflections
like those anchored waterscapes that wander, alter, in the Taff,
hour by hour, as light slants down a different shade.

Illusory, too, that lost dark playground after rain,
the noise of trams, gunshots in what they once called Tiger Bay.
Only real this smell of ripe, damp earth when the sun comes out,
a mixture of pungencies, half exquisite and half plain.

No sooner than I'd arrived the other Cardiff had gone,
smoke in the memory, these but tinned resemblances,
where the boy I was not and the man I am not
met, hesitated, left double footsteps, then walked on.

Sunday Evening

Loved not for themselves those tenors who sing
arias from 'Aïda' on horned, tinny
gramophones – but because they take a man back
to a half forgotten thing.

We, transported by this evening loaded
with a song recorded by Caruso,
recall some other place, another time,
now charmingly outmoded.

What, for wrong motives, too often is approved
proves we once existed, becomes mere flattery
– then it's ourselves whom we are listening to,
and, by hearing, we are moved.

To know, haunted, this echo too will fade
with fresh alliteration of the leaves,
as more rain, indistinct, drags down the sky
like a sense of gloom mislaid.

Dear classic, melodic absences
how stringently debarred, kept out of mind,
till some genius on a gramophone
holes defences, breaks all fences.

What lives in a man and calls him back
and back through desolate Sunday evenings?
Indescribable, oh faint generic name:
sweet taste, bitter lack.

As I was Saying

Yes, madam, as a poet I *do* take myself seriously,
and, since I have a young, questioning family, I suppose
I should know something about English wild flowers:
the shape of their leaves, when this and that one grows,
how old mythologies attribute strange powers
to this or that one. Urban, I should mug up anew
the pleasant names: Butterbur, Ling, and Lady's Smock,
Jack-by-the-Hedge, Cuckoo-Pint, and Feverfew,
even the Stinking Hellebore – all in that W. H. Smith book
I could bring home for myself (inscribed to my daughter)
to swot, to know which is this and which that one,
what honours the high cornfield, what the low water,
under the slow-pacing clouds and occasional sun
of England.

But no! Done for in the ignorant suburb,
I'll drink Scotch, neurotically stare through glass
at the rainy lawn, at green stuff, nameless birds,
and let my daughter, madam, go to nature class.
I'll not compete with those nature poets you advance,
some in country dialect, and some in dialogue
with the country – few as calm as their words:
Wordsworth, Barnes, sad John Clare who ate grass.

Olfactory Pursuits

Often, unobserved, I smell my own hand.
I am searching for something forgotten.
I bang the door behind me, breathing in.

I think that a bitter or candied scent
is like a signpost pointing backwards
on which is writ no place and no distance.

So I walk towards a Verulamium,
your ruins or my ruins. The sun's ambushed:
fleeing on the ground the same, large shadow.

Look up. There's no smell to the colour blue.
The wind blew it right through the spaces
between clouds. Christ, what is it I'm after?

I dream, without sleeping, of things obscure,
of houses and streets and temples deserted
which, if once visited, I don't recall.

Here are a few stones instead of a wall,
and here broken stones instead of a house.
Hopelessly, with odours I conjoin.

My footfall echoes down old foundations,
buried mosaics, tomb tablets crumbled,
flints in the grass, your ruins or my ruins.

A man sniffs the back of his own hand,
moistens it with his mouth, to sniff again,
to think a blank; writes, 'The odour of stones.'

Pathology of Colours

I know the colour rose, and it is lovely,
but not when it ripens in a tumour;
and healing greens, leaves and grass, so springlike,
in limbs that fester are not springlike.

I have seen red-blue tinged with hirsute mauve
in the plum-skin face of a suicide.
I have seen white, china white almost, stare
from behind the smashed windscreen of a car.

And the criminal, multi-coloured flash
of an H-bomb is no more beautiful
than an autopsy when the belly's opened –
to show cathedral windows never opened.

So in the simple blessing of a rainbow,
in the bevelled edge of a sunlit mirror,
I have seen, visible, Death's artifact
like a soldier's ribbon on a tunic tacked.

Hunt the Thimble

Hush now. You cannot describe it.

Is it like heavy rain falling,
and lights going on, across the fields,
in the new housing estate?

Cold, cold. Too domestic, too
temperate, too devoid of history.

Is it like a dark windowed street at night,
the houses uncurtained, the street deserted?

Colder. You are getting colder,
and too romantic, too dream-like.
You cannot describe it.

The brooding darkness then,
that breeds inside a cathedral
of a provincial town in Spain?

In Spain, also, but not Spanish.
In England, if you like, but not English.
It remains, even when obscure, perpetually.
Aged, but ageless, you cannot describe it.
No, you are cold, altogether too cold.

Aha – the blue sky over Ampourias,
the blue sky over Lancashire for that matter . . .

You cannot describe it.

. . . obscured by clouds?
I must know what you mean.

Hush, hush.

Like those old men in hospital dying,
who, unaware strangers stand around their bed,
stare obscurely, for a long moment,
at one of their own hands raised –

which perhaps is bigger than the moon again –
and then, drowsy, wandering, shout out, 'Mama'.

Is it like that? Or hours after that even:
the darkness inside a dead man's mouth?

No, no, I have told you:
you are cold, and you cannot describe it.

A Night Out

Friends recommended the new Polish film
at the Academy in Oxford Street.
So we joined the ever melancholy queue
of cinemas. A wind blew faint suggestions
of rain towards us, and an accordion.
Later, uneasy, in the velvet dark
we peered through the cut-out oblong window
at the spotlit drama of our nightmares:
images of Auschwitz almost authentic,
the human obscenity in close-up.
Certainly we could imagine the stench.

Resenting it, we forgot the barbed wire
was but a prop and could not scratch an eye;

those striped victims merely actors like us.
We saw the Camp orchestra assembled,
we heard the solemn gaiety of Bach,
scored by the loud arrival of an engine,
its impotent cry, and its guttural trucks.
We watched, as we munched milk chocolate,
trustful children, no older than our own,
strolling into the chambers without fuss,
while smoke, black and curly, oozed from chimneys.

Afterwards, at a loss, we sipped coffee
in a bored espresso bar nearby
saying very little. You took off one glove.
Then to the comfortable suburb swiftly
where, arriving home, we garaged the car.
We asked the au pair girl from Germany
if anyone had phoned at all, or called,
and, of course, if the children had woken.
Reassured, together we climbed the stairs,
undressed together, and naked together,
in the dark, in the marital bed, made love.

Not Adlestrop

Not Adlestrop, no – besides, the name
hardly matters. Nor did I languish in June heat.
Simply, I stood, too early, on the empty platform,
and the wrong train came in slowly, surprised, stopped.
Directly facing me, from a window,
a very, *very* pretty girl leaned out.

When I, all instinct,
stared at her, she, all instinct, inclined her head away
as if she'd divined the much married life in me,
or as if she might spot, up platform,
some unlikely familiar.

For my part, under the clock, I continued
my scrutiny with unmitigated pleasure.
And she knew it, she certainly knew it, and would not
glance at me in the silence of not Adlestrop.

Only when the train heaved noisily, only
when it jolted, when it slid away, only *then*,
daring and secure, she smiled back at my smile,
and I, daring and secure, waved back at her waving.
And so it was, all the way down the hurrying platform
as the train gathered atrocious speed
towards Oxfordshire or Gloucestershire.

In Llandough Hospital

'To hasten night would be humane,'
I, a doctor, beg a doctor,
for still the darkness will not come –
his sunset slow, his first star pain.

I plead: 'We know another law.
For one maimed bird we'd do as much,
and if a creature need not suffer
must he, for etiquette, endure?'

Earlier, 'Go now, son,' my father said,
for my sake commanding me.
Now, since death makes victims of us all,
he's thin as Auschwitz in that bed.

Still his courage startles me. The fears
I'd have, he has none. Who'd save
Socrates from the hemlock,
or Winkelried from the spears?

We quote or misquote in defeat,
in life, and at the camps of death.
Here comes the night with all its stars,
bright butchers' hooks for man and meat.

I grasp his hand so fine, so mild,
which still is warm surprisingly,
not a handshake either, father,
but as I used to when a child.

And as a child can't comprehend
what germinates philosophy,
so like a child I question why
night with stars, then night without end.

Photograph and White Tulips

A little nearer please. And a little nearer
we move to the window, to the polished table.
Objects become professional: mannequins
preening themselves before an audience. Only
the tulips, self-absorbed, ignore the camera.

All photographs flatter us if we wait
long enough. So we awkwardly Smile please
while long-necked tulips, sinuous out of the vase,
droop over the polished table. They're entranced
by their own puffed and smudgy reflections.

Hold it! Click. Once more! And we smile again
at one who'll be irrevocably absent.
Quick. Be quick! the tulips, like swans, will dip
their heads deep into the polished table
frightening us. Thank you. And we turn thinking

What a fuss! Yet decades later, dice thrown,
we'll hold it, thank you, this fable of gone
youth (was that us?) and we shall smile please
and come a little nearer to the impetuous
once-upon-a-time that can never be twice.

(Never never be twice!) Yet we'll always recall
how white tulips, quick quick, changed into swans
enthralled, drinking from a polished table.
As for those white petals, they'll never fall
in that little black coffin now carrying us.

2

Poems 1967–1989

Mysteries

At night, I do not know who I am
when I dream, when I am sleeping.

Awakened, I hold my breath and listen:
a thumbnail scratches the other side of the wall.

At midday, I enter a sunlit room
to observe the lamplight on for no reason.

I should know by now that few octaves can be heard,
that a vision dies from being too long stared at;

that the whole of recorded history even
is but a little gossip in a great silence;

that a magnesium flash cannot illumine,
for one single moment, the invisible.

I do not complain. I start with the visible
and am startled by the visible.

Peachstone

I do not visit his grave. He is not there.
Out of hearing, out of reach. I miss him here,
seeing hair grease at the back of a chair
near a firegrate where his spit sizzled,
or noting, in the cut-glass bowl, a peach.

For that night his wife brought him a peach,
his favourite fruit, while the sick light glowed,
and his slack, dry mouth sucked, sucked, sucked,
with dying eyes closed – perhaps for her sake –
till bright as blood the peachstone showed.

A New Diary

This clerk-work, this first January chore
of who's in, who's out. A list to think about
when absences seem to shout, Scandal! Outrage!
So turning to the blank, prefatory page
I transfer most of the names and phone tags
from last year's diary. True, Meadway, Speedwell,
Mountview, are computer-changed into numbers,
and already their pretty names begin to fade
like Morwenna, Julie, Don't-Forget-Me-Kate,
grassy summer girls I once swore love to.
These, whispering others and time will date.

Cancelled, too, a couple someone else betrayed,
one man dying, another mind in rags.
And remembering them my clerk-work flags,
bitterly flags, for all lose, no-one wins,
those in, those out, *this* at the heart of things.
So I stop, ask: whom should I commemorate,
and who, perhaps, is crossing out my name now
from some future diary? Oh my God,
Morwenna, Julie, don't forget me, Kate.

The Death of Aunt Alice

Aunt Alice's funeral was orderly,
each mourner correct, dressed in decent black,
not one balding relative berserk with an axe.
Poor Alice, where's your opera-ending?
For alive you relished high catastrophe,
your bible Page One of a newspaper.

You talked of typhoid when we sat to eat;
Fords on the M4, mangled, upside down,
just when we were going for a spin;
and, at London airport, as you waved us off,
how you fatigued us with 'metal fatigue',
vague shapes of Boeings bubbling under seas.

Such disguises and such transformations!
Even trees were but factories for coffins,
rose bushes decoys to rip boys' eyes with thorns.
Sparrows became vampires, spiders had designs,
and your friends also grew SPECTACULAR,
none to bore you by dying naturally.

A. had both kidneys removed in error
at Guy's. 'And such a clever surgeon too.'
B., one night, fell screaming down a liftshaft.
'Poor fellow, he never had a head for heights.'
C., so witty, so feminine, 'Pity
she ended up in a concrete-mixer.'

But now, never again, Alice, will you utter
gory admonitions as some do oaths.
Disasters that lit your eyes will no more
unless, trembling up there, pale saints listen
to details of their bloody martyrdoms,
all their tall stories, your eternity.

In the Theatre

(A true incident)

'Only a local anaesthetic was given because of the blood pressure problem. The patient, thus, was fully awake throughout the operation. But in those days – in 1938, in Cardiff, when I was Lambert Rogers' dresser – they could not locate a brain tumour with precision. Too much normal brain tissue was destroyed as the surgeon crudely searched for it, before he felt the resistance of it . . . all somewhat hit and miss. One operation I shall never forget . . .'

(Dr Wilfred Abse)

Sister saying – 'Soon you'll be back in the ward,'
sister thinking – 'Only two more on the list,'
the patient saying – 'Thank you, I feel fine';
small voices, small lies, nothing untoward,
though, soon, he would blink again and again
because of the fingers of Lambert Rogers,
rash as a blind man's, inside his soft brain.

If items of horror can make a man laugh
then laugh at this: one hour later, the growth
still undiscovered, ticking its own wild time;
more brain mashed because of the probe's braille path;
Lambert Rogers desperate, fingering still;
his dresser thinking, 'Christ! Two more on the list,
a cisternal puncture and a neural cyst.'

Then, suddenly, the cracked record in the brain,
a ventriloquist voice that cried, 'You sod,
leave my soul alone, leave my soul alone,' –
the patient's dummy lips moving to that refrain,
the patient's eyes too wide. And, shocked,

Lambert Rogers drawing out the probe
with nurses, students, sister, petrified.

'Leave my soul alone, leave my soul alone,'
that voice so arctic and that cry so odd
had nowhere else to go – till the antique
gramophone wound down and the words began
to blur and slow, '. . . leave . . . my . . . soul . . . alone . . .'
to cease at last when something other died.
And silence matched the silence under snow.

Cousin Sidney

Dull as a bat, said my mother
of cousin Sidney in 1940 that time he tried
to break his garden swing, jumping on it,
size 12 shoes – at fifteen the tallest boy
in the class, taller than loping Dan Morgan
when Dan Morgan wore his father's top hat.

Duller than a bat, said my father
when hero Sidney lied about his age
to claim rough khaki, silly ass;
and soon, somewhere near Dunkirk,
some foreign corner was forever Sidney
though uncle would not believe it.

Missing not dead please God, please,
he said, and never bolted the front door,
never string taken from the letter box,
never the hall light off lest his one son
came home through a night of sleet
whistling, We'll meet again.

Aunt crying and raw in the onion air
of the garden (the unswinging empty swing)
her words on a stretched leash
while uncle shouted, Bloody Germans.
And on November 11th, two howls
of silence even after three decades

till last year, their last year,
when uncle and aunt also went missing,
missing alas, so that now strangers
have bolted their door and cut the string
and no-one at all (the hall so dark)
waits up for Sidney, silly ass.

White Coat, Purple Coat

White coat and purple coat
  a sleeve from both he sews.
That white is always stained with blood,
  that purple by the rose.

And phantom rose and blood most real
  compose a hybrid style;
white coat and purple coat
  few men can reconcile.

White coat and purple coat
  can each be worn in turn
but in the white a man will freeze
  and in the purple burn.

The Stethoscope

Through it,
over young women's tense abdomens,
I have heard the sound of creation
and, in a dead man's chest, the silence
  before creation began.

Should I
pray therefore? Hold this instrument in awe
and aloft a procession of banners?

Hang this thing in the interior
    of a cold, mushroom-dark church?

            Should I
kneel before it, chant an apophthegm
from a small text? Mimic priest or rabbi,
the swaying noises of religious men?
    Never! Yet I could praise it.

            I should
by doing so celebrate my own ears,
by praising them praise speech at midnight
when men become philosophers;
    laughter of the sane and insane;

            night cries
of injured creatures, wide-eyed or blind;
moonlight sonatas on a needle;
lovers with doves in their throats; the wind
    travelling from where it began.

A Winter Visit

Now she's ninety I walk through the local park
where, too cold, the usual peacocks do not screech
and neighbouring lights come on before it's dark.

Dare I affirm to her, so agèd and so frail,
that from one pale dot of peacock's sperm
spring forth all the colours of a peacock's tail?

I do. But she like the sibyl says, 'I would die';
then complains, 'This winter I'm half dead, son.'
And because it's true I want to cry.

Yet must not (although only Nothing keeps)
for I inhabit a white coat not a black
even here – and am not qualified to weep.

So I speak of small approximate things,
of how I saw, in the park, four flamingoes
standing, one-legged on ice, heads beneath wings.

The Doctor

Guilty, he does not always like his patients.
But here, black fur raised, their yellow-eyed dog
mimics Cerberus, barks barks at the invisible,
so this man's politics, how he may crawl
to superiors, do not matter. A doctor must care
and the wife's on her knees in useless prayer,
the young daughter's like a waterfall.

Quiet, Cerberus! Soon enough you'll have a bone
or two. Now, coughing, the patient expects
the unjudged lie: 'Your symptoms are familiar
and benign' – someone to be cheerfully sure,
to transform tremblings, gigantic unease,
by naming like a pet some small disease
with a known aetiology, certain cure.

So the doctor will and yes he will prescribe
the usual dew from a banana leaf; poppies and
honey too; ten snowflakes or something whiter
from the bole of a tree; the clearest water
ever, melting ice from a mountain lake;
sunlight from waterfall's edge, rainbow smoke;
tears from eyelashes of the daughter.

X-ray

Some prowl sea-beds, some hurtle to a star
and, mother, some obsessed turn over every stone
or open graves to let that starlight in.
There are men who would open anything.

Harvey, the circulation of the blood,
and Freud, the circulation of our dreams,
pried honourably and honoured are
like all explorers. Men who'd open men.

And those others, mother, with diseases
like great streets named after them: Addison,
Parkinson, Hodgkin – physicians who'd arrive
fast and first on any sour death-bed scene.

I am their slowcoach colleague, half afraid,
incurious. As a boy it was so: you know how
my small hand never teased to pieces
an alarm clock or flensed a perished mouse.

And this larger hand's the same. It stretches now
out from a white sleeve to hold up, mother,
your X-ray to the glowing screen. My eyes look
but don't want to; I still don't want to know.

Pantomime Diseases

When the fat Prince french-kissed Sleeping Beauty
her eyelids opened wide. She heard applause,
the photographer's shout, wedding-guest laughter.
Poor girl – she married the Prince out of duty
and suffered insomnia ever after.

The lies of Once-upon-a-Time appal.
Cinderella seeing white mice grow into horses
shrank to the wall – an event so ominous
she didn't go to the Armed Forces Ball
but phoned up Alcoholics Anonymous.

Snow White suffered from profound anaemia.
The genie warned, 'Aladdin, you'll go blind,'
when that little lad gleefully rubbed his lamp.
The Babes in the Wood died of pneumonia.
D. Whittington turned back because of cramp.

Shy, in the surgery, Red Riding Hood undressed
– Dr Wolff, the fool, diagnosed Scarlet Fever.
That Jill who tumbled down has wrecked her back,
that Puss-in-Boots has gout and is depressed
and one bare bear gave Goldilocks a heart attack.

When the three Darling children thought they'd fly
to Never-Never Land – the usual trip –
their pinpoint pupils betrayed addiction.
And not hooked by Captain Hook but by
that ponce, Peter Pan! All the rest is fiction.

Imitations

In this house, in this afternoon room,
my son and I. The other side of glass
snowflakes whitewash the shed roof and the grass
this surprised April. My son is sixteen,
an approximate man. He is my chameleon,
my soft diamond, my deciduous evergreen.

Eyes half closed he listens to pop forgeries
of music – how hard it is to know – and perhaps
dreams of some school Juliet I don't know.
Meanwhile, beyond the bending window,
gusting suddenly, despite a sky half blue,
a blur of white blossom, whiter snow.

And I stare, oh immortal springtime, till
I'm elsewhere and the age my cool son is,
my father alive again (I, his duplicate),
his high breath, my low breath, sticking to the glass
while two white butterflies stumble, held each
to each as if by elastic, and pass.

Last Words

Splendidly, Shakespeare's heroes,
Shakespeare's heroines, once the spotlight's on,
enact every night, with such grace, their verbose deaths.
Then great plush curtains, then smiling resurrection
to applause – and never their good looks gone.

The last recorded words too
of real kings, real queens, all the famous dead,
are but pithy pretences, quotable fictions
composed by anonymous men decades later,
never with ready notebooks at the bed.

Most do not know who they are
when they die or where they are, country or town,
nor which hand on their brow. Some clapped-out actor may
imagine distant clapping, bow, but no real queen
will sigh, 'Give me my robe, put on my crown.'

Death scenes not life-enhancing,
death scenes not beautiful nor with breeding;
yet bravo Sydney Carton, bravo Duc de Chavost
who, euphoric beside the guillotine, turned down
the corner of the page he was reading.

And how would I wish to go?
Not as in opera – that would offend –
nor like a blue-eyed cowboy shot and short of words,
but finger-tapping still our private morse, '. . . love you,'
before the last flowers and flies descend.

Phew!

Do you know that Sumerian proverb
'A man's wife is his destiny'?
But supposing you'd been here,
this most strange of meeting places,
5000 years too early? Or me,
a fraction of a century too late?
No angel with SF wings
would have beckoned,
'This way, madam, this way, sir.'

Have you ever, at a beach,
aimed one small pebble
at another, thrown high, higher?

And though what ends
happily
is never the end,
and though the secret is
there's another secret always,

because this, because that,
because on high the Blessed
were playing ring-a-ring-o'-roses,
because millions of miles below,
during the Rasoumovsky,
the cellist, pizzicati,
played a comic, wrong note,
you looked to the right, luckily,
I looked to the left, luckily.

Horse

You can't quite
identify it
the long straight road
unsignposted
zipping between hedges
to a scandalously
gorgeous sunset.
As you look closer
shading your eyes
with your right hand
vigilant you'll see
the visitant
the white horse
half way down it.

Do you remember?
Your father drove the car
the family squabbling
this way years ago
many a time
this Roman road
that's empty now
but for the distant
truant pink horse
with a barely
visible
red shadow
racing towards
the signals of sunset.

War-high in the sky
vapour trails fatten
and you know again
the common sense
of déjà vu. Perhaps
someone far from home
should be playing
a mouth organ
a melody slow
and sad and wanton
a tune you've heard
but can't quite say
as the purple horse
surprises the sunset.

And you close your eyes
trying to name it all.
But you recall only
the day's small prose
certain queachy things
what the office said
what the office did
as the sunset goes
as the black horse goes
into the darkness.
And you forget
how from the skin
below your thumbnail
your own moon rises.

In the Holiday Inn

After the party I returned to the hotel.
The room was too hot so I took off my coat.

It was January but I turned down the thermostat.
I took off my shirt but I was still too hot.

I opened the window, it was snowing outside.
Despite all this the air began to simmer.

The room had a pyrexia of unknown origin.
I took off my trousers, I took off my shorts.

This room was a cauldron, this room was tropical.
On the wall, the picture of willows changed

to palm trees. In the mirror I could see the desert.
I stood naked in my socks and juggled

with pomegranates. I offered offerings
that soon became burnt. This was some holiday.

I took off one sock and read the bible.
They were cremating idols, sacrificing oxen.

I could feel the heat of their fiery furnace.
I could hear those pyromaniacs chanting.

I could smell the singed wings of cherubim.
I took off the other sock and began to dance.

Like sand the carpet scalded my twinkling feet.
Steam was coming out of both my ears.

I was King David dancing before the Lord.
Outside it was snowing but inside it was Israel.

I danced six cubits this way, six cubits that.
Now at dawn I'm hotter than the spices of Sheba.

What shall I do? I shall ask my wise son,
Solomon. Where are you Solomon?

You are not yet born, you do not know
how wise you are or that I'm your father

and that I'm dancing and dancing.

Case History

'Most Welshmen are worthless,
an inferior breed, doctor.'
He did not know I was Welsh.
Then he praised the architects
of the German death-camps –
did not know I was a Jew.
He called liberals, 'White blacks',
and continued to invent curses.

When I palpated his liver
I felt the soft liver of Goering;
when I lifted my stethoscope
I heard the heartbeats of Himmler;
when I read his encephalograph
I thought, '*Sieg heil, mein Führer.*'

In the clinic's dispensary
red berry of black bryony,
cowbane, deadly nightshade, deathcap.
Yet I prescribed for him
as if he were my brother.

Later that night I must have slept
on my arm: momentarily
my right hand lost its cunning.

Encounter at a Greyhound Bus Station

If belief, like heaven, lies beyond the facts
what serpent flies with an ant between its teeth?

asked the over-bearded man with closed eyes.
Who are they who descend when they ascend?

this kabbalist with eyes closed, asked.
Are all men in disguise except those crying?

And what exists in a tree that doesn't exist,
its eggs looted by creatures not yet created?

★ ★ ★ ★

Partial to paradoxes, disliking riddles,
I hummed and I hawed, I advocated

the secrets of lucidity. Then said,
Some talk in their sleep, very few sing.

Abruptly, the unwashed one opened his lids,
rattled one coin inside a tin.

I looked into the splendour of his eyes
and laid my hand upon my mouth.

★ ★ ★ ★

Then he scoffed: You are like the deaf man
who knows nothing of music or of dance

yet blurts out, observing musicians play
and dancers dance – Stupid, how stupid

those who carve the air this way and that,
who blow out their cheeks and make them fat,

who mill about, clutch and maul each other
as if the very earth and all would fall.

⋆ ⋆ ⋆ ⋆

And what could I, secular, say to that?
That I'm deaf to God but not in combat?

Cool pretensions of reason he'd dismiss
and if I threw stones he'd build a house.

Yet I begged: Dare to reveal, sir, not conceal;
not all, translucent, lose authority.

Fool, he replied, I'm empty, feed my tin,
which I did, of course, when the bus came in.

A Wall

in a field in the County of Glamorgan.
You won't find it named in any guidebook.
It lies, plonk, in the middle of rising ground,
forty-four paces long, high as your eyes,
it begins for no reason, ends no place.
No other walls are adjacent to it.
Seemingly unremarkable, it's just there,
stones of different sizes, different greys.

Don't say this wall is useless, that the grass
on the shadow side is much like the other.
It exists for golden lichens to settle,
for butterflies in their obstacle race
chasing each other to the winning post,
for huddling sheep in a slanting rainfall,
for you to say, 'This wall is beautiful.'

The Origin of Music

When I was a medical student
I stole two femurs of a baby
from The Pathology Specimen Room.
Now I keep them in my pocket,
the right femur and the left femur.
Like a boy scout, I'm prepared.
For what can one say to a neighbour

when his wife dies? 'Sorry'?
Or when a friend's sweet child
suffers leukaemia? 'Condolences'?
No, if I should meet either friend
or stricken neighbour in the street
and he should tell me, whisper to me,
his woeful, intimate news,
wordless I take the two small femurs
from out of my pocket sadly
and play them like castanets.

A Prescription

Sweet-tempered, pestering
young man of Oxford
juggling with ghazals,
tercets, haikus, tankas,
not to mention villanelles,
terzanelles and rondelets;
conversant with the phonetic
kinships of rhyme, assonance
and consonance; the four
nuances of stress, the three
junctions; forget now
the skeltonic couplet,
the heroic couplet, the split

couplet, the poulter's measure;
speak not of englyn
penfyr, englyn milwr;
but westward hasten
to that rising, lonely ground
between the evening rivers,
the alder-gazing rivers,
Mawddach and Dysynni.

Let it be dark when, alone,
you climb the awful mountain
so that you can count the stars.
Ignore the giant shufflings
behind you – put out that torch! –
the far intermittent cries
of the nocturnal birds
– if birds they are –
their small screams of torture.
Instead, scholar as you are,
remark the old proverb
how the one who ascends
Cadair Idris at night
comes back in dawn's light
lately mad or a great poet.
Meanwhile, I'll wait here
in this dull room of urine-
flask, weighing-machine,
examination-couch, X-ray screen,
for your return (triumphant
or bizarre) patiently.

The Wife of Columbus

After I made love
to the wife of Christopher Columbus
I woke up. Later, over breakfast,
I consulted a map.
Had I not kissed a birthmark
on the soft inside of her right thigh,
a birthmark that resembled
the contours of an island,
familiar but forgotten?
And yet, not necessarily an island.
Error? Columbus thought he'd reached
the spice-rich coast of India.

I have visited, in real daylight,
Columbus, capital of Ohio,
observed Doric buildings
under island-clouds. I have walked
past the Institute of the Blind
questing for something lost, once seen;
also past the Penitentiary
and the Catholic Cathedral
where tall and short women entered,
some hiding their faces
as she did once when the three ships
set sail from the quay at Palos.

Error. I should have journeyed
to a place not on my itinerary –
Columbus, Georgia, perhaps,
and walked all the moody afternoon
beside the Chattahoochee river

searching for a sign;
or Columbus, Indiana, say,
and waited like one asleep
at its junction of railways
for a train of many windows –
with so many sitting skeletons,
so many skulls staring out.

White Balloon

Dear love, Auschwitz made me
more of a Jew than ever Moses did.
But the world's not always with us.
Happiness enters here again tonight
like an unexpected guest
with no memory of the future either;

enters with such an italic emphasis,
jubilant, announcing triumphantly
hey presto and here I am and opening
the June door into our night living room
where under the lampshade's ciliate
an armchair's occupied by a white balloon.
As if there'd been a party.

Of course, Happiness, uninhibited,
will pick it up, his stroking thumb
squeaking a little as he leads us to the hall.
And we shall follow him, too,
when he climbs the lit staircase
towards the landing's darkness,
bouncing bouncing the white balloon
from hand to hand.

It's bedtime; soon we must dream
separately – but what does it matter now
as the white balloon is thrown up high?
Quiet, so quiet, the moon above Masada
and closed, abandoned for the night,
the icecream van at Auschwitz.

Brueghel in Naples

'About suffering they were never wrong,
The Old Masters . . .' – W. H. Auden

Ovid would never have guessed how far
and Father's notion about wax melting, bah!
It's ice up there. Freezing.
Soaring and swooping over solitary altitudes

I was breezing along (a record I should think)
when my wings began to moult not melt.
These days, workmanship, I ask you.
Appalling.

There's a mountain down there on fire
and I'm falling, falling away from it.
Phew, the sun's on the horizon
or am I upside down?

Great Bacchus, the sea is rearing
up. Will I drown? My white legs
the last to disappear? (I have no trousers on.)
A little to the left the ploughman,
a little to the right a galleon,
a sailor climbing the rigging,
a fisherman casting his line,
and now I hear a shepherd's dog barking.
I'm that near.

Lest I leave no trace
but a few scattered feathers on the water
show me your face, sailor,
look up, fisherman,
look this way, shepherd,
turn around, ploughman.
Raise the alarm! Launch a boat!

My luck. I'm seen
only by a jackass of an artist
interested in composition, in the green

tinge of the sea, in the aesthetics
of disaster – not in me.

I drown, bubble by bubble,
(Help! Save me!)
while he stands ruthlessly
before the canvas, busy busy,
intent on becoming an Old Master.

3

Later Poems

St Valentine's Night

Eros, immutable archer, one eye closed,
you let your arrows fly. It was St Valentine's
night, I remember. For me the first time.
The Cardiff moon was flirting with a cloud, its light discreet,
and I with a box of Black Magic chocolates
and she with such a healthy appetite.

Homage to Eros! Slow and sensual the sweet
unwrapping, the soft-centred she coming into sight.
St Valentine, himself, would have been up
to make her, with her fallen party dress
rustling on the rug like classy chocolate paper.

Be with me still, jubilant Eros, life-saver,
necessary ally. The other gods only wound
the world and scowling Thanatos keeps trying
to recite the 11th commandment: Thou shalt die.
It was St Valentine's night, I remember.
You plucked your great bow then, Eros. Pluck it now.

Marzipan. Cherry Liqueur. Turkish Delight.

1989–2009

Condensation on a Windowpane

1

I want to write something simple,
something simple, few adjectives,
ambiguities disallowed.

Something old-fashioned:
a story of Time perhaps
or, more daringly, of love.

I want to write something simple
that everyone can understand,
something simple as pure water.

But pure water
is H_2O
and that's complicated
like steam, like ice, like clouds.

2

My finger squeaks on glass.
I write JOAN
I write DANNIE.
Imagine! I'm a love-struck
youth again.

I want to say something
without ambiguity.
Imagine! me, old-age pensioner
wants to say something

to do with love and Time,
love that's simple as water.

But long ago we learnt
water is complicated,
is H_2O, is ice, is steam, is cloud.

Our names on the window
begin to fade.
Slowly, slowly.
They weep as they vanish.

Beautiful Dead Poets

She spoke of Garcia Lorca murdered;
Hernandez dying in a Franco prison;
Mayakovsky's suicide; how Mandelstam
jumped through the window of a hospital;
Celan and Levi in the Nazi Death Camps.
'Beautiful dead poets, all of them,' said she,
in the delight of enthusiasm.

Behind her, a dark mahogany table
that once had the girth of a lofty tree;
a vase of deep red, drooping lovely things –

aged tulips – untimely ripped from the earth;
and, by the window, a canary caged
because it sang so beautifully.

Cricket Ball

1935, I watched Glamorgan play
especially Slogger Smart, free
from the disgrace of fame, unrenowned,
but the biggest hit with me.

A three-spring flash of willow
and suddenly, the sound of summer
as the thumped ball, alive, would leave
the applauding ground.

Once, hell for leather, it curled
over the workman's crane
in Westgate Street
to crash, they said, through a discreet
Angel Hotel windowpane.

But I, a pre-war boy,
(or someone with my name)
wanted it, that Eden day,

to scoot around the turning world,
to mock physics and gravity,
to rainbow-arch the posh hotel
higher, deranged, on and on, allegro,
(the Taff a gleam of mercury below)
going, going, gone
towards the Caerphilly mountain range.

Vanishings! The years, too, gone like change.
But the travelling Taff seems the same.
It's late. I peer at the failing sky
over Westgate Street
and wait. I smell cut grass.
I shine an apple on my thigh.

Touch Wood

Come, let us praise wood
no longer agrestial.
Not the trillions of coffins
but wood within a living house,
the quietude of an empty bookcase,
the loneliness of scattered chairs –
the metamorphosis

of trees, shrubs, bushes, twigs.
Doors particularly, upstairs, downstairs,
whatever their disposition,
welcoming, half open,
or secretively shut.

It does not matter.
Delightful the craftsmanship
of their lintels,
so comely, so pleasant,
like the repeated oblongs
of windowframes, upstairs, downstairs,
like the serenity of windowsills
that carry vases, flower-pots.
And who could not respond
to the utilitarian elegance
of a wide staircase
rising from a parquet floor?

What a history wood has,
what old echoing stories
in the random museum of the mind:
the gopher ark of Noah
floating high above the mountains;
the huge, staring Trojan horse;
Diogenes's fat barrel;
Horatius's one-way bridge
that fell into the Tiber;
King Arthur's Round Table –

all these relics lost forever
like Jesus's insensate Cross.

Sometimes I think we should construct
in the garden of a living house
an idol of various woods:
head of Lombardy Poplar,
trunk of reliable Oak,
arms of Elm and Pine,
hands of Lime and Plane,
legs of Birch and Beech,
feet of grainy Sycamore
and genitals (of course, discreet)
of musty Fig tree, untidy Fir
and the droopy Weeping Willow.

November nights when we're asleep,
when unbuttoned winds shake the house,
what the spirit of the house
if not the spirit of the forest?
What replies if not primal wood,
dryad-ghost and Daphne-creak,
wild cries of wood awakening?
We, stern-faced as mourners, slumber on,
carry in dream the golden bough
from some black forgotten tree
of the windless underworld
back to the leaf-strewn morning.

Ghosting for Mayakovsky

(*His suicide note*)

1

It's long past one and you must be asleep.
The quiet night's astonished by all the stars.
Why wake you now with a telegram like thunder?

So many thoughts of mystery the night can bring.
Dear lŏve, our love boat's on the rocks. Its sails
wrenched from the mast. No use in adding up the cost,
we're quits; no need to weigh our hearts and hurts
upon the scales. 'No Life without you,' once I said,
and now the strokes of Two thud down like heads from blocks.

Our story's over, iconoclast. I'm lost. I'm through.
No need to wake you with a telegram like thunder.
Art's imperative will make these lines come true.

2

Once I drew the Queen of Hearts,
now I'm dealt another card. A club. A two.
Once forbidden love lit up like paper burning
then it charred.

Once with verse of lightning and half in song
I told a daisy and the world
you loved me, you love me not,
and how worthless life unfurled would be
without you – like a single shoe.
I'll not limp along.

I'm shot. I'm through.
Queen of Hearts, O Queen of Hearts,
the imperatives of Art insist,
the lies of Art come true.

Thankyou Note

for the unbidden swish of morning curtains
you opened wide – letting sleep-baiting shafts
of sunlight enter to lie down by my side;
for adagio afternoons when you did the punting
(my toiling eyes researched the shifting miles of sky);
for back-garden evenings when you chopped the wood
and I, incomparably, did the grunting;
(a man too good for this world of snarling
is no good for his wife – truth's the safest lie);

for applauding my poetry, O most perceptive spouse;
for the improbable and lunatic, my darling;
for amorous amnesties after rancorous rows,
like the sweet-nothing whisperings of a leafy park
after the blatant noise of a city street,
(exit booming cannons, enter peaceful ploughs);
for kindnesses the blind side of my night-moods;
for lamps you brought in to devour the dark.

O Taste and See

Because of a kiss on the forehead
in the long Night's infirmary,
through the red wine let light shine deep.

Because of the thirty-six just men
that so stealthily roam this earth
raise high the glass and do not weep.

Who says the world is not a wedding?
Couples, in their oases, lullabye.
Let glass be full before they sleep.

Toast all that which seems to vanish
like a rainbow stared at, those bright
truant things that will not keep;

and ignorance of the last night
of our lives, its famished breathing.
Then, in the red wine, taste the light.

At the Albert Hall

Anarchic dissonances first, so that
somewhere else a lonely scarecrow shivers
in a winter field. A mortician's crow
perches on its head. It begins to snow.
They bring the scarecrow indoors. They feed it
with phosphorus so it should glow at night.
A great orchestra's tuning-up is ghost talk.

The wand! Then the sudden tamed silence of
a cemetery. Who dares to blackly cough?
Threatened, the conductor raises both arms,
an invisible gun pressed to his back.
Listen. And they speak of the sweet psalmist
of Israel, of 200 loaves of bread
and of 100 bundles of raisins.

Lament of Heledd

(based on a fragment of a 9th-century Welsh saga poem)

I

I had four brothers. A pike upholds the head
of noble Cynddylan. The corn is red.

I had four brothers. Cynon and Gwiawn
butchered in the straw, their swords not drawn.

Four brothers I had. Vague, hesitant Gwyn
last to fall. Through his neck a javelin.

When will this brute night end? Where shall I go?
Morning's mortuary will be kitchen for the crow.

II

Cynddylan's Hall is dark tonight.
The stone stairs lead nowhere. No candle glows
behind the lower then the higher windows.

Cynddylan's Hall is dark tonight
and dark the smoke rising from its ruin.
Slain, slain, are Cynddylan and all our kin.

Cynddylan's Hall is dark tonight,
its great roof burnt down, I can see the stars.
Curse those Englishmen, their bloody wars.

Cynddylan's Hall is dark tonight.
No orison is wailed to harp or lute.
O ghost brothers, your sister's destitute.

Cynddylan's Hall is dark tonight,
its silence outrageous. I shall go mad.
I smell skeletons. O blood of my blood.

Cynddylan's Hall is dark tonight.
Should I live on? I am no heroine.
O Cynddylan, Cynon, Gwiawn, and Gwyn.

A Heritage

A heritage of a sort.
A heritage of comradeship and suffocation.

The bawling pit-hooter and the god's
explosive foray, vengeance, before retreating
to his throne of sulphur.

Now this black-robed god of fossils
and funerals,
petrifier of underground forests
and flowers,
emerges with his grim retinue
past a pony's skeleton, past human skulls,
into his half-propped up, empty, carbon colony.

Above, on the brutalized,
unstitched side of a Welsh mountain,
it has to be someone from somewhere else
who will sing solo

not of the marasmus of the Valleys,
the pit-wheels that do not turn,
the pump-house abandoned;

nor of how, after a half-mile fall
regiments of miners' lamps
no longer, midge-like,
rise and slip and bob.

Only someone uncommitted,
someone from somewhere else,

panorama-high on a coal-tip
may jubilantly laud
the re-entry of the exiled god
into his shadowless kingdom.

C'est La Vie Politique

When promised
a subtle perfume,
tactful dilutions
of musk, civet, ambergris,

expect 'a human error',
a veritable gasworks.
Dry in the polluted air
plain H_2S.

When promised
a hundred piece orchestra –
Berlioz, Mahler –
a tune on a comb.

When a Queen's diamond,
a snail's shell;
when a King's golden crown,
a funny paper hat.

Consider Mr Maltby,
fancy tailor, who agreed
a suicide pact
with his wife.

She did not falter;
he was unable.
He propped her up
naked in the bath.

Night after night
brought lit candles
into that bathroom
where he quietly dined,

faithfully choosing
her favourite dishes,
fish mainly – turbot, trout –
gently removing the bones.

Souls

'After the last breath, eyelids must be closed
quickly. For eyes are windows of the soul
– that shy thing which is immortal. And none
should see its exit vulnerably exposed,'

proclaimed the bearded man on Yom Kippur.
Grown-ups believed in the soul. Otherwise
why did grandfather murmur the morning prayer,
'Lord, the soul Thou hast given me is pure'?

Near the kitchen door where they notched my height
a mirror hung. There I saw the big eyes
of a boy. I could not picture the soul
immaterial and immortal. A cone of light?

Those two black zeros the soul's windows? Daft!
Later, at medical school, I learnt of
the pineal gland, its size a cherry-stone,
vestige of the third eye, and laughed.

But seven colours hide in light's disguise
and the blue sky's black. No wonder Egyptians
once believed, in their metamorphosis,
souls soared, became visible: butterflies.

Now old, I'm credulous. Superstition clings.
After the melting eyes and devastation
of Hiroshima, they say butterflies, crazed,
flew about, fluttering soundless things.

A Letter from Ogmore-by-Sea

Goodbye, 20th Century.
What should I mourn?
Hiroshima? Auschwitz?
Our friend, Carmi, said,
'Thank forgetfulness
else we could not live;
thank memory
else we'd have no life.'

Goodbye, 20th Century.
What shall I celebrate?
Darling, I'm out of date:
even my nostalgia
is becoming history.
Those garish, come-on posters
outside a cinema,
announce the Famous
I've never heard of.
So many other friends, too,
now like Carmi, have joined
a genealogy of ghosts.

But here, this mellow evening,
on these high cliffs I look down
to read the unrolling
holy scrolls of the sea. They are
blank. The enigma is alive
and, for the Present, I boast,
thumbs in lapels, I survive.

Delightful Eros
still hauls Reason along
zig-zag on a taut leash.
I'm still unsettled by
the silence in framed pictures,
foreground and background;
or the mastery of music
over mind. And I hail
the world within a word.
I do not need to be
a fabulist like Iolo
who, from this same coast,
would see seven sails
where there was but one.

Goodbye, 20th Century,
your trumpets and your drums,
your war-wounds still unhealed.
Goodbye, I-must-leave-you-Dolly,
goodbye Lily Marlene.
Has the Past always a future?
Will there always be
a jackboot on the stair,
a refugee to roam?
A man with no roots is lost
like the darkness in the forest
and it costs 100 years
for a hiding place
to become a home.

Now secular strangers come
sealed in Fords and Nissans,
a congregation of cars,
to this opening estuary
so various, so beautiful, so old.
The tide is out.
And from the sleeping reeled –
in sea – not from
the human mind's vexed fathoms –
the eternal, murderous,
fanged Tusker Rock is revealed.

Child Drawing in a Hospital Bed

Any child can open wide
the occult doors of a colour
naively to call, 'Who's there?'
For this sick girl drawing
outstep invisible ones
imprisoned everywhere.
Wasp on a windowpane.

Darkest tulip her head bends,
face white as leukaemia,
till the prince in his tower,
on parole from a story,

descends by royal crayon
and, thrilled, stays half an hour.
Wasp on a windowpane.

Birds of Rhiannon, pencilled,
alight to wake the dead –
they do not sing, she rubs them out,
they smudge into vanishings,
they swoop to Nowhere
as if disturbed by a shout.
Wasp on a windowpane.

Omens. Wild astrologies whirl:
sun and moon begin to soar.
Unlikely that maroon sky
green Christmas trees fly through
– doctors know what logic's for.
Tell me, what is magic for?
Wasp on a windowpane.

Now penal-black she profiles
four eerie malformed horses,
nostrils tethered to the ground.
Unperturbed, the child attends
for one to uplift its neck
and turn its death's head round.
Wasp on a windowpane.

Just a Moment

As my wife arranges the lilac in a vase
I think how for years I've stared from this window
at that garden tree so stark it seemed ashamed;
or as now in May, proud – dressed to the nines,
rustling its green silks and in stately bloom.

I've stood here observing Time's sorcery,
the petroleum sunset behind its branches,
the midges energetic above the grass,
or the rising moon a phoenix in its high leaves.

I have grown old watching such things
and thought how a poet's late adagios
like those of Beethoven (*Muss es sein?*)
should say more about the seasons of fate
than the years have wings and the hours pass.

But now I'm attentive to the window itself
and, for a moment, I've cracked it again, trespassed
into the half-mad timeless world that is still
where I am not old nor will be older –
the tip of my tongue against the glass,
the chill touch of it, the nothing taste of it,
until I breathe in the jubilant Yes
and mortally precarious fragrance of lilac
my wife has just placed upon the windowsill.

Terrible Angels

One bedtime, my father showed me his war medals,
their pretty coloured ribbons, and told me
the other story about the angels of Mons,
that élite and puissant expedition from God:
how first their invisible presence caused horses
to bolt and flocks of meat-snatching birds to rise,
circle around and around like a carousel.

But war coarsens (he said) even genteel angels.
When they spoke it was the silence of gas, amen;
when they sang it was shrapnel striking helmets;
then, finally, soldiers' prayers and soldiers' screams
thrilled the cold angels to steal the muskets
of the dead, to become stealthily visible,
bold and bloodthirsty, true facsimiles of men.

(My father, invalided home, was told
he knew more about angels than was healthy.)

The Relic

(A variation of Ewald Osers' translation of 'Paradise Lost' by J. Seifert)

I, Jaroslav Seifert,
opened the pages of the Bible
and my mother, my expert,
taught me the cognominal codes
of the Old Testament women.

Adah signifies rich ornament;
Ophrah, gentle mare of the red deer;
Abigail, true source of joy
(Come out to play, come out to play);
and Naamah, one whose beauty
could lead the open-mouthed angels astray.

But when, years later, blow after blow,
they dragged away the Jews,
their children scared and helpless,
not one of us dared
to call out a modest 'No'.

Tamar signifies palm tree
with its dates, its sugar and wine;
Zilpah, a little droplet
of such a little drop;
Jemima means peaceful dove, pure and divine;
and Tirzah, pleasure-giving (as in love).

But they dragged away the Jews.
Tallest behind the barbed wire
Jecholiah, half-skeleton, his big eyes
so soon to feed the flies. Such a joke!
His name signifies 'The Lord is All-Powerful'.

Rachel means warm woolly ewe-lamb;
Delilah, ringlets, falling tresses,
their darknesses and their points of light;
Deborah, a swarm of honey bees;
Esther, starbright starbright.

And I almost forgot, Shoshana.
Oh Shoshana means rose,
the only flower left to us on this earth
from the Eden that was.

The Tailor

eyes peculiarly large still
his frightened face ethereal

soft-voiced he said little
except the yellow star
they gave him
was of very cheap material

The Story of Lazarus

After the war he settled in kindly Cardiff
his English uncertain, his Welsh not at all.
For three years a clerk who hardly said a word.

Then, accusingly, he showed us the number
on his arm, spoke of how he had survived
in his chemistry, the sudden sound of
his heartbeat. Each stark detail. We were shocked.

Week after week this man's monstrous story
heard in Whitchurch, Llandaf, Canton, Cathays,
in pubs and clubs – The Three Elms, The Conway,
The Golden Shark, the Post House, the Moat House;
told even to Cardiff's patient statues:
John Batchelor, Lloyd George, Nye Bevan.

We closed our eyes till we, too, became stone.
So he whispered his dark story to our children
and years later to our children's children.
Soon they merely nodded, eager to join
the procession banging its way outside
to the Firework Display above Roath Park,
the oompha, oompha, down the street fading.

Prufrock at the Seaside

A beautiful woman should be looking at me
as I think big thoughts and stare at the sea.

On this cliff I feel like a movie star
but without my glasses I can't see far.

Perhaps if I had a little more hair
and owned a Rolls-Royce like a millionaire

those bikini ladies mincing by
would, like greedy bees, to my honey fly.

Once I wore the bottoms of my trousers rolled
but my legs are thin and feel the cold.

'You should have married Maisie,' said her friend,
'personified contentment, love without end.'

Pectoral young men play football on the beach
under circling seagulls crying each to each.

'Maisie sweet,' I'd said, 'marry me' but she turned sour,
looked as cheerful as Schopenhauer.

Afterwards, forever, for the sake of my health
I thought it best to mate with myself.

A small boy throws a stone to skim the sea,
a black dog runs after it uselessly.

I remember the sandwiches my mother made,
my teeth grinding sand, red bucket and spade

and in the car going home we all would sing
'Stormy Weather'. Me as Sinatra or Bing.

The football players' shadows run and grow long.
Suddenly the prom's coloured lamps come on.

Look! That scandalous couple. He's stroking her breast.
Oh King David, voyeur, I see them undressed.

The sundown's punctual, the clouds are dyed.
I'm no Don Juan – but what if I'd tried?

I still dream of Maisie, rose with a thorn,
she a queen to lead me, I her willing pawn.

The waves lash on but the sea's in its chains.
The beach becomes desolate. The dog remains.

The Yellow Bird

I do not want it
the witchcraft song of the yellow bird,
nor this room of whisperings
as the slanting rain punctual
pelts against the windowpane.

I do not want it
the heavy brocaded curtains motionless,
her face in profile, Egyptian-like,
unsmiling, emotionless,
staring into the sorry street.

I do not want it
these mirrors without reflections,
these clothes ritually torn, rage in rags,
this piano-lid closed,
a coffin of music.

They say the yellow bird in anger
can only sing sweetly. Not so.

It sang piercingly
in the garden, at the cool of the day,
when Adam, fearful, hid among the bushes.

It sang raucously,
turning its dreadful, juridic beak
in the ululating caves of the troglodytes.

And it sang eerily
in the courts of Osiris, the sunsetter,
the lord of the dead, the judge of souls.

There are no frontiers, my friend, for the yellow bird.

It sang, hovering above the fire,
its wings beating just above the fire,
before the warriors ate their prisoners.

Later, it sang the glory of the celestial
for St Paul in his trance
to become his pet bird, his ally and harbinger.

It sings still at the River Styx
as the ferry crosses and the dog barks;
and in the evening ghost-mists
of long ago deserted battlefields.

It sings in every hospital at 3 a.m.
the song of incurable darkness.

I do not want it
the four coal-black limousines
now hushing their way
to a crematorium.

I do not want it
the overt horror in the beauty
of the wreath.

I do not want it, I do not want it,
the congregation that dare not weep,
the weariness of the God-man,

his mechanical laudation,
his secret ennui of disbelief.

Sing noiselessly, yellow bird,
if sing you must. Or sleep.

1945, 2001

Why Angels and Unicorns Disappeared

When first the celestial orchestra played
decorously the angels began to dance.

This was the time when the moon unmuzzled
glowed twice more luminously than now.

But wanton Azazel, the angel of Vice,
unhooked his nice masterpiece wings, displayed,

enticed daft angels to swig double-strength nectar,
deft angels to juggle the fruits of Paradise.

Hallelujah! Hallelujah! That unquiet night
(such an orgy) half the angels got laid

and their pet unicorns ran riot, began to bite,
called for pale maidens to make life rosier.

Their randy horns grew and grew. Some howled at
the moon, some crapped on the ambrosia.

Soon the Archangel's police arrived, blew
whistles for music to cease, moonlight to fade

and foolishly fed the frenetic unicorns
tinned human flesh, calming pesticides.

Later, the angels ate all the unicorns,
suffered CJD. Not one of them survived.

No Lazarus

At the time of the Resurrection
not one person rose up
from the cemeteries of London.
But, at Marylebone Road,
a procession of clothed dummies
streamed out of Madame Tussaud's,
arms raised, wild, shouting Hallelujah.

The Archbishop of Canterbury
and other official sources
denied a computer error.

Enemies

Remembering dirty deeds and verbal blows
Heine said he'd be glad to forgive his enemies
once their bodies were swinging on a gallows.

I have an affinity with Heine.
To forgive my enemies is my quest.

But no need for them to swing on gallows
pecked to meat by magpies and by crows.
A Garden of Rest will do – one well-cared
for, well-aired – fragrance of cut grass,
gravel pathways, elaborate headstones.

No expense spared. I'll pay.
(Such charity they say is blessed.)
I'm so longing to be virtuous.
I'm so impatient to pardon them.

Religion

Blithely, the stranger on the soapbox claimed
that God was created when they prayed;
that, at night, mystic lights magnified the church,
the abandoned one at the top of the hill.

'Go, at midnight,' he said, 'hear organ music
and ecstatic voices as pure as angels'.'
So they obeyed and climbed the hill of lampposts,
afraid they might find the proof they hoped for.

But the windows were dark and no voices sang.
The doors opened to the muteness of stone
and, relieved, they fell to their knees and prayed.

Between 3 and 4 a.m.

1

Wakeful at 3 a.m.
near the frontiers of Nothing
it's easy, so easy
to imagine (like William Blake)
an archaic angel standing
in a cone of light
not of this world;

easy at the cheating hour
to believe an angel cometh
to touch babies' skulls,
their fontanelles,
deleting the long memory
of generations –
(only prodigies not visited);
easy to conceive angel-light
bright as that sudden,
ordinary window
I saw at midnight
across the road
before the drawing
of its blind.

2

Once, another presence
also nocturnal, oneiric,
secretive, in disguise,

waiting behind
an opening Seder door.

'No,' says the child. 'Gone.'
Framed in that black oblong,
nobody.

(A shadow flies
when a light is shone.)

Was childhood real?
Did a stallion attempt
to mount a mare
painted by Apelles?
Did Greek workmen hear
the exiled statue sob
when carried to
Lord Elgin's ship?
The mystery named
is not the mystery caged.

Even a night-scene
may be an illusion
like an afternoon harbour
viewed through sunglasses,
the light forged
to a moon-tortured sea.

3

I was visited once, once only, elsewhere,
near a lake, near an oak,
near a weeping willow tree and thorn,
one summertime, out of time, in England,
during the cosmic love-making hour
when day and night shyly intermingle,

when day, entranced, does not know what or who
and night, ecstatic, is not itself entirely
till the slow coming of the stars.
But now, weeping willow tree and thorn,
there's only the dread of Nothing.

(Nothing, say the kabbalists
is more real than nothing.)

It's 4 a.m. already and cold
and quiet, quiet as a long
abandoned battlefield.
Late to trawl, net full of holes,
the grounded darkness
for what, naturally, can never be told.

(The unutterable, at best, becomes music.)

No, it's time to hold the silence found
on one side
with the right hand,

the silence on the other
with the left,
then to pull, pull, pull,

till silence tears without a sound.

Welsh Valley Cinema, 1930s

In The Palace of the slums,
from the Saturday night pit,
from an unseen shaft of darkness
I remember it: how, first, a sound
took wing grandly; then the thrill
of a fairground sight – it rose,
lordly stout thing, boasting
a carnival of gaudy-bright,
changing colours while wheezing out
swelling rhonchi of musical asthma.

I hear it still, played with panache
by renowned gent, Cathedral Jones,
'When the Broadway Baby Says Goodnight
it's Early in the Morning' – then he and it
sank to disappear, a dream underground.

Later, those downstairs, gobbing silicosis
(shoeless feet on the mecca carpet),
observed a miracle – the girl next door,
a poor ragged Goldilocks,
dab away her glycerine tears
to kiss cuff-linked Cary Grant
under an elegance of chandeliers.
(No flies on Cary. No holes in *his* socks.)

And still the Woodbine smoke swirled on
in the opium beam of the operator's box
till THE END – of course, upbeat.
Then from The Palace, the damned Fall,
the glum, too silent trooping out
into the trauma of paradox:
the familiar malice of the dreary,
unemployed, gas-lamped street
and the striking of the small Town's clocks.

Things

Nichts ist mir zu klein, und ich lieb es trotzdem und mal' es auf Goldgrund und gross . . .

R. M. Rilke

The strange, changing intimacy
of closely examined things

that studious painters know.
Dead caterpillars take wings.

Keepsake pebbles, exiled shells,
looted from some holiday shore,
this mysterious giant key
that opens no familiar door.

So many things not wanted,
so many things outgrown:
a red uncomfortable chair,
an outdated telephone,
a vase in detestable taste
once won at an Easter fair.

A shiny suit, a discarded shoe,
clocks that no longer tick,
a broken musical box –
Frère Jacques, dormez-vous?

So many things finished and old
that make Time visible;
and nothing too useless
or graceless, or diminished
that cannot be tenderly painted
on a background of gold.

The Jeweller

That rainy night, the Poetry Reading over, he drove me
 home.
'As a doctor you must have seen many a bloody sight,
– but you poets no longer delight in the serenity of things.
If you had my job would you write of jewels fit for kings:
the delicate yellow-tinted topaz of Brazil, maybe,
or the wine-hued topaz sometimes set in queenly rings?'

Then I, at the traffic lights, saw the joy of stealthy colours
on the black wet tarmac. (First you see them, then you
 don't.)
Not the terminal jaundice in Freda's eyes, nor the wings
of rosacea on Goronwy's face, but the gold alloy
tiara that Clytemnestra wore at Delphi
and the heart-stopping rubies Agamemnon stole from Troy.

North

Between the black tree trunks
the snow, white as a frightened eye,
and still the snow-shocked road
looped North, always North.

In a stinging panic the disorder
of flying snowflakes resumed,
blown by the wind that howled
and hated us. We looked back

for our footprints but
they no longer followed;
so much blank, ruffled napery
and we seemingly anaesthetised.

The sweat froze on our foreheads
and, suddenly, we saw it
for one sublime moment only,
the white horse in the snowstorm.

Trembling, awake with otherness,
we did not shout at the wind.
Then all was as before. Silently
we tracked North again. Always North.

Praise May Thither Fly

Let us praise the blaspheming Old Masters
though some in greed lied and cheated,
and some, unsavoury, beat their wives,
or strangely let their wives beat them!

And some, perhaps, once or twice a year
at sundown thought the monstrous shadow following
momentarily was not their own.

All, all sycophants of magic,
all flea bitten, mosquito bitten, lice infested,
smelly practitioners of the absurd
who by indirections found directions out
– this ordinary man, that ordinary man,
one minute a sinner, the next a seer.

Such accidents of craft! Such hauntings!
As if they had heard a robust shout
in the wind –
some believing what they did not hear.

There – at the very centre of the circle
where work becomes worship,
such danger to themselves
when they, half-tranced, amazed themselves

retrieving from the Invisible
(some dared not sign their names)
crazed saints, hovering haloes,
the stout, ruminating Virgin
with her hefty baby, Jesus,
and, leering amongst the attentive angels,
the monstrous one they quickly painted out.

Shobo

He hardly knew a single English word
and was too much in pyrexial sloth
to throw 16 kola nuts from his right hand
to his left. The interpreter grumbled
that he worried about your clay-red tie.
This colour, it seemed, invoked the wrath
of Shopanna, Lord of the Open Spaces.

You were not trusted. You knew nothing of
his gods, their shrines, those tall pillars of mud,
nor of the dread power of the earth-spirits.
He felt himself to be perversely cursed
and could not send for the babalawo
– the priest who kept water in his house
but preferred, sometimes, to bathe in blood.

You were too rational in your white coat,
unable to offer analgesic words
in the right order. And no heaven-sent
antibiotic could dispatch a curse.
So away he wasted, eyes ever more distant.
Pyrexia of unknown origin, you said.
He died. Status lymphaticus, you said.

And the post-mortem revealed little cause.
A thymic death? Guilt and his fey belief
in a vile incubus? Sometimes I think
of Shobo at night, mystery's habitat,
where a man may fancy he hears a footfall
on the stairs becoming faint, fainter,
ever more distant, till not heard at all.

Rilke's Invitation

Come by the sun-hammered route
where the bordering grass has no colour.
Passing the red barn look out for

the old fallen oak with a hollow in it.
Its gaping bark, since once upon a time,
has been secretly collecting water.

To drink from it would be indelicate,
too open, too bold. I have been refreshed
by dipping my wrists down through its cold
bland pristine silence till my mind's alive
like sparkling light-haunting water.

Do come. When you arrive, celibate friend,
I'll be content to rest my hand
first on your shoulder – and then, gently,
upon your breast's responding pressure.

Lucky

(*for Max*)

Lucky, lover of balls, one at her paws,
brown eyes patient, expectant, impatient.
Go on, pick it up you nitwit, she seems to say,
throw this one, bowl it overhead, a googly if
you like.

No! I don't want to hear again your story
of the daft sincere girl in the pavilion
who reckoned you're a great bowler
because you hit the bat every time.

And don't drone on about evening sunlight
cloud-shadows chasing a red ball to the boundary,
the ripple of disconnected applause
like money shaken in a charity box.

And don't tell me about the big winter-egg either
prematurely flying towards the tall H.
Just pick this one up, this one, yeh, and
forget the soccer ball which your left foot
squinted the wrong side of the post.

And don't even think about
those upper-class wooden guys on horseback
who thwack their hockey sticks
at a round apology of a thing
I can't even get my teeth into.

And definitely, definitely, disremember
the golf ball that with your usual help

arced and vanished into legend,
sniffed out, you'd probably have it,
by that blind, clever-dick, clapped-out Argus
while Penelope's noisy claque
jumped and jostled for a beach ball,
played catch to the sound of music.

Book stuff! Give it a rest, old nitwit.
Just throw this ball and above all abjure the one
that you, with such a haunted, insomniac look,
hurl too often through the gone years
to where I, Lucky, can't run and run,
tail Time-wagging, to proudly bring it back.

Ovid's Wish

I'd rather be in hell with one woman
than in heaven with all those sexless angels.

Corinna may deceive me and then we
quarrel – but oh what reconciliations!

True, Desire's lantern burns dimly sometimes
yet with a little oil it soon flares up.

You know how it is: a horse bolts suddenly
and, helpless, the rider tugs at the reins.

Or a yacht is driven back from the shore
when its bold sails are caught in gusts of wind.

Well, Cupid's arrows know their own way home.
They feel more at home in me than in their quiver!

Life's on lease. Why settle for eight hours' sleep
and ignore delightful flighty Cupid?

Sleep's a rehearsal for undying Death.
There's time enough for nights of peace. So shoot

on, with one eye closed, mischievous boy:
let your arrows seek my heart for ever.

A Letter to Stanley Moss in New York

Dear 'Colleague in the art' your invitation
to your son's wedding in Fiesole
arrived on one of those grey pensioner days
when the apple lies worm-eaten in the wooden bowl.
I had awakened to a September day
that would have rusted on a railway siding
and left no visiting card behind.
But now, Fiesole-thoughts irradiate my mind
with an avalanche of jubilant sunlight.

Alas, I can't be with you. I'm committed
to present my lecture on Death at Llanbadarn
for the resurrected Merrie Wales Society.
Hurrah, though, I say whenever two dare to marry.
It's such a brisk signal of optimism, isn't it?
Like Eve saying Au revoir on leaving Paradise.

You write that you've ordered your centaurs
and your Russian dancers to Fiesole.
No father could do more. A price above rubies.
I wish I could send my platoon of corybants
but they outrageously absconded years ago
to the fertility goddess's bunker.
Instead, I offer your son my only advice:
Hilarity is not welcome at the breakfast table.

Also I've penned a note to my agent in Florence
to supply bride and groom with a dozen jars
of my good, deodorized, golden eye-ointment.
I trust this gift will not be misunderstood.
You know how that can be. Our Z and your Z.

The final letter of the alphabet, by the way,
I always think, is on its knees praying
with its back to the abyss. Do you agree?

Meanwhile, I'll post the ecstatic couple
(let their life be all honey and nightingales)
a photostat of my lecture on Death.
Please keep a slice of wedding cake for me.

All Things Bright and Beautiful

Faint, reassuring for some, the bells outside.
This is England. Religion not quite dead!
Besides, a fat daft bee zigzagging this room
(windows open) seems to mumble a Sunday matin
and I recall how my least of religion
and my little Latin have been scrubbed out
like chalk from Brother Vincent's 6th Form blackboard.

Once Sir thrust his Roman beak towards me,
the bleak crucifix above his head.
'You say you never pray, boy? Never?'
All those fustian words by rote. Affluent beggars
falling to their knees in the gloom of a church
and a god in agony upon a wall.
I shambled. Was this the Inquisition?

I would not convert. Fear is the hasp of Religion.
I'd be a hero, write 'amo' in wine
and ignore the Hand no man can grasp.
Let the priest rage, kindle lightning and thunder,
thrash the cane-rod on his long black skirt.
'All I believe in, Brother, is wonder.'

And I thought of the odd idiot boy, Rhys,
on the high Wenallt range, looking down,
suddenly crying out, 'Oh, well done God.'

But now this room is quiet. The bee has blundered
into the garden and soon Religion's bells will cease.

At Caerleon

This shadowy spring evening,
in these ruins of Caerleon,
I hear the alarm of distant shouts.
Soon the skinhead knights
of The Round Table gang appear.
Bored, they horse around, frab,
and throw empty cans of beer
at each other.

The scarred and tattooed
loudest lout
seems to be their King.
The long knife in his buskin
is as keen as Arthur's sword.

Deprived, they bully language
into oaths
until, suddenly, together,
as if a starting gun had sounded,
the outcast, broiling yobs depart
to seek another gang to cull.

A smear of blood on a silken flag,
a golden crown on a decaying skull,
a lust for heroes,
this is where the legends start.
And I'm alone at last,
can lose my reason,
sit upon a stone and play
(paper on a comb) a mournful tune
from an imagined country

that would break an exile's heart,
or summon silhouettes like phantoms
who were coming,
came and now have passed.

At the Concert

Only yesterday while walking on Ogmore cliffs
one listless sheep gave me the yellow eye.
Its jaws moved sideways, munching over and over.
The same old grass. Same old flavour.

I strolled inland and saw the big brown horse
in Lol's sloping field. It stood utterly still.
When I returned it hadn't moved an inch.
It must have been as bored as any statue.

And here's a pretty Miss next to me, motionless.
She'll sit in Row G unawakened by
the conductor's sudden convulsions till
the very last note like a Prince's kiss.

And how's your life? Static too? Do you wait,
as I do, numb, for something to happen
until it happens? If so, join the queue.
It stretches all the way to the Old People's Home.

I'm thinking all this, I mean about the sheep
and the horse, about you and about me
as I pretend to listen to Klump's new free-form
yawn-fecund 'Machine of Dissonances'.

What else can I do except try not to cough
while my cat back home squats in my chair
unmolested, deigning to blink now and then –
at the blank TV screen? I wish I was there

staring through the window at the pear tree's
serene magnificence, its masquerade of snow.
But now Miss is on her feet applauding.
The concert's over. Happily, I shout 'Bravo'.

On the Coast Road

This ash-end of the year, too short of light,
the grumpy afternoon closes down
and a bossy wind summons, like a conductor,
choirs of ghosts to the telegraph wires.

Soon the roofs of Ogmore recede out of sight
as I walk on awake in the wrong weather.
Ahead, a seagull squeals, bullied off course,
and sheep scrum behind stone-armoured walls.

Tons of air! And nobody on this coast road,
and nobody on the beach below where
the thaumaturge sea thrashes the rocks
and hey-hey presto, fakes fountains of snow.

Down there, on that rock's pulpit, my father
fished
till his own days grew shorter. Now, briefly,
this road leads to the Past. Is it the scolding wind
that makes my teeth ache and my eyes water?

At the old, shut farmhouse, I meet a boozy gang
in fancy dress. The man in a white sheet
holds up, on a pole, the skull of a horse.
The Mari Lwyd! I blink. They vanish of course

and the graffito I, as a boy, once chalked
on the ruined barn beyond this farmhouse
has vanished too: STRAIGHT ON FOR THE FUTURE.
Quick, bird, quick, present winds shake the lamp-posts

into staring light. As if pursued, a tin can
buckets past me, scrapes the bleak macadam,
its off-key tinkle diminishing plaintively
with each forward struggling step I take.

Phone Call at Ogmore-by-Sea

At 3 a.m., the hour of the rising Dead,
Hello, Hello? No-one spoke.

Beyond the limits of the ordinary
a stranger would have stood, skull to toe,
transfixed in the doorway
like a lit enlarged X-ray film!

Hello? Hello? I wait and know
the intimidation of silence.

Discharged
from the lunatic asylum of sleep,
now alert, adrenal, I explore
the moonstruck window.

Outside, the sighing, fussy
surge of the sea swarming up
the unpeopled, pebbled shore.

Certain nights the house creaks
and the nearer I move to the dead hour
the smaller I become.

I've eaten my prunes, Daddy.
I've taken my cod-liver oil.

The clock's disarmed.
The night-bird is flying to the moon

and wind and cloud play lighting tricks
above the inebriated-dancing sea
that flaunts mock silver on its blacks.

A Marriage

Love, almost three score licit years have passed
(racist fools said our marriage would not last)
since our student days, honeysuckle nights,
when you'd open the jammed sashed window
above the dark basement flat and I, below,
would be an urgent, athletic Romeo.

Remember when I hacked my shin and swore
and you put an exclamation mark to your lips
because of the German landlady's law:
NO VISITORS AFTER 10 P.M.
She kept castrating instruments for men!

Up the creaking stairs Indian file, the door
closed, you'd play before one amorous word
a Louis Armstrong record or another diverting disc
lest something of our nothings would be heard.

Oh the stealth of my burglar's exit through the dark,
the landlady's dog, that we called Wagner,

alert, anti-Semitic, lifting its ears
to rehearse a virtuoso chilling bark.

I hear its echo still at the front garden gate,
down the lamplit street, faint, through the hurrying years
to where we are, in sickness and in health,
in perdurable love, ageing together,
lagging somewhat, slowly running late.

The Malham Bird

(For Joan)

That long summer a clarity of marvels
yet no morning News announced the great world
had been reinvented and we were new,
in love – you a Gentile and I a Jew!

Dear wife, remember our first illicit
holiday, the rented room, the hidden beach
in Wales, the tame seagull that seemed a portent,
a love message, as if Dafydd's ghost had sent it?

After our swim we lay on our shadows naked,
more than together, and saw high in the blue
two chalk lines kiss and slowly disappear.
Then the friendly gull swooped down, magnified, near.

Now, three grandchildren later, I think of
a black feathered bird, the malham of Eden,
how it took advice, closed its eyes resolute,
when others singing pecked forbidden fruit;

and how, of all the birds, it was not banished
but stayed, lonely, immortal, forever winging
over the vanished gardens of Paradise.

With Compliments

Dear, if I had a small legacy from Croesus
I would purchase – please do not argue –
that painting of gladioli by Soutine
you so admired. But in a waking fit
of realism I've bought
this bunch of robust-red,
radiantly alive upstanding gladioli
from The Corner Flower Stall instead.

Lachrymae

(i) The Accident

I crawled from the noise of the upturned car
and the silence in the dark began to grow.
I called out her name again and again
to where neither words nor love could go.

(ii) Later

I went to her funeral.
I cried.
I went home that was not home.

What happened cannot keep.
Already there's a perceptible change of light.
Put out that light. Shades
lengthen in the losing sun.
She is everywhere and nowhere
now that I am less than one.

Most days leave no visiting cards behind
and still consoling letters make me weep.
I must wait for pigeon memory
to fly away, come back changed
to inhabit aching somnolence
and disguising sleep.

(iii) Winter

What is more intimate
than a lover's demure whisper?

Like the moment before Klimt's *The Kiss*.
What more conspiratorial
than two people in love?

So it was all our eager summers
but now the yellow leaf has fallen
and the old rooted happiness
plucked out. Must I rejoice when
teardrops on a wire turn to ice?

Last night, lying in bed,
I remembered how, pensioners both,
before sleep, winter come,
your warm foot suddenly
would console my cold one.

(iv) Swan Song

Night fairground music
and, like kids, we sat astride
daft horses bouncing on
the lit-wide Merry-Go-Round
to swagger away, serene,
old lovers hand in hand.

Now, solemn, I watch
the spellbound moon again,
its unfocused clone drowned
in Hampstead's rush-dark pond
where a lone swan sings
without a sound.

2005

After the Memorial

Some spoke of her unostentatious beauty:
she, passionate moralist, Truth's sweet secretary.
No-one heard the sobbing of the angels.

Well, I have my own weeping to do.
(If angels could weep they would become human.)
I lived her life and she lived mine –
not only in the easy valleys of Pretend
where bosky paths descend to lakes where no swan
is singular (and fish ignore the hunched Angler)

but here where the uphill road to happiness
has ordinary speed limits,
and still the revelation is
that there can be such a thing

until it must yield to a dead end.

So now our marriage book is drowned
(there seemed magic in it)
and she is both manifest and concealed –
manifest because I see her everywhere,
concealed because she is nowhere to be found.

The Revisit

This scene too beautiful, it seemed a fake:
the unlikely sky, the drowning sunset lake.
With you by my side, did I dream awake?

God's spacious canvases always amaze
even when lucid colours become uncertain greys.
There was nothing else we could do but praise.

Yet darkness, like dread, lay within the scene
and you said, 'Just like music that seems serene.'
(Mozart stared at green till he became the green.)

And there, above the lake, of course unsigned,
its surface hoofed with colour by the wind
were great windows between clouds, fires behind,

as if from Angel wars. Such April bloodshed!
The wide sky-fires flared and their glitter-red
sparks cooled to scattered stars instead.

Now I, bereaved, like the bruised sky in disrepair,
a shadow by my side, hear a far owl's thin despair.
I stare at colour till I am the stare.

The gradual distance between two stars is night.
Ago, love, we made love till dark was bright.
Now without you dark is darker still and infinite.

The Violin Player

Too often now, half somnolent, I would go
like Yeats to a fortunate Lake Isle where
unblemished water-lilies never die,
and no solitary swan floats by
from everlasting to everlasting.

And in the tranquil orchard of this Isle
I'd plunder such paradisial apples
that Cezanne could have painted – apples
no bird would have dared to peck at,
fraudulent but beautiful.

Yes, I would go there rapt, recreant,
and stay there because, sweet, you're not here
till, self-scolded, I would recollect
my scruffy, odorous Uncle Isidore
(surely one of the elect) who played

unsettling, attenuated music
long after a string had snapped,
whose beard bent down to interject,
'Little boy, who needs all the lyric strings?
Is the great world perfect?'

Valediction

In this exile people call old age
I live between nostalgia and rage.
This is the land of fools and fear.
Thanks be. I'm lucky to be here.

4

Longer Poems

The Smile Was

one thing I waited for always
after the shouting
after the palaver
the perineum stretched to pain
the parched voice of the midwife
                                Push! Push!
and I can't and the rank
sweet smell of the gas
and
                                I can't
as she whiffed cotton wool
inside her head
as the hollow stones of gas
dragged
                    her
                          down
from the lights above
to the river-bed, to the real stones.
                                Push! Push!
as she floated up again
muscles tensed, to the electric
till the little head was crowned;
and I shall wait again
for the affirmation.

For it is such:
that effulgent, tender, satisfied
smile of a woman
who, for the first time,
hears the child crying the world
for the very first time.

That agreeable, radiant smile –
no man can smile it
no man can paint it
as it develops without fail,
after the gross, physical, knotted,
granular, bloody endeavour.
   Such a pure spirituality, from all that!
It occupies the face
and commands it.
                Out of relief
you say, reasonably thinking of the reasonable,
swinging, lightness of any reprieve,
the joy of it, almost helium in the head.

                So wouldn't you?
And truly there's always the torture of the unknown.
There's always the dream of pregnant women,
blood of the monster in the blood of the child;
and we all know of generations lost
like words faded on a stone,
of minds blank or wild with genetic mud.
                And couldn't you
smile like that?

Not like that, no, never,
not with such indefinable
dulcitude as that.
And so she smiles
with eyes as brown as a dog's
or eyes blue-mad as a doll's
it makes no odds

whore, beauty, or bitch,
it makes no odds
illimitable chaste happiness
in that smile
as new life-in-the-world
for the first time cries the world.
No man can smile like that.

2

No man can paint it.
Da Vinci sought it out
yet was far, far, hopelessly.
Leonardo, you only made
Mona Lisa look six months gone!

I remember the smile of the Indian.
I told him
                    Fine, finished,
you are cured
and he sat there smiling sadly.
Any painter could paint it
the smile of a man resigned
saying
                    Thank you, doctor,
you have been kind
and then, as in melodrama,
                    How long
have I to live?
The Indian smiling, resigned,
all the fatalism of the East.

So one starts again, also smiling,
All is well
you are well, you are cured.
And the Indian still smiling
his assignations with death
still shaking his head, resigned.
Thank you
for telling me the truth, doctor.
Two months? Three months?

And beginning again
and again
whatever I said, thumping the table,
however much I reassured him
the more he smiled the conspiratorial
smile of a damned, doomed man.

Now a woman, a lady, a whore,
a bitch, a beauty, whatever,
the child's face crumpled
as she becomes the mother,
she smiles differently, ineffably.

3

As different as
the smile of my colleague,
his eyes reveal it,
his ambiguous assignations,
good man, good surgeon,
whose smile arrives of its own accord
from nowhere

like flies to a dead thing
when he makes the first incision.
Who draws a line of blood
across the soft, white flesh
as if something beneath,
desiring violence, had beckoned him;
who draws a ritual wound,
a calculated wound
to heal – to heal,
but still a wound –
good man, good surgeon,
his smile as luxuriant
as the smile of Peter Lorre.

So is the smile of my colleague,
the smile of a man
secretive behind the mask.

The smile of war.

But the smile, the smile
of the new mother,
what
  an extraordinary
    open thing
      it is.

4

Walking home tonight I saw
an ordinary occurrence
hardly worth remarking on:

an unhinged star, a streaking gas,
and I thought how lovely
destruction is when it is far.
Ruined it slid
on the dead dark towards fiction:
its lit world disappeared
phut, through one punched hole or another,
slipped unseen down the back of the sky
into another time.

Never,
not for one single death
can I forget we die with the dead,
and the world dies with us;
yet
in one, lonely,
small child's birth
all the tall dead rise
to break the crust of the imperative earth.

No wonder the mother smiles
a wonder like that,
a lady, a whore, a bitch, a beauty.
Eve smiled like that
when she heard Seth cry out Abel's dark,
earth dark, the first dark
eeling on the deep sea-bed,
struggling on the real stones.
Hecuba, Cleopatra, Lucretia Borgia,
Annette Vallon smiled like that.

They all, still, smile like that,
when the child first whimpers like a seagull
the ancient smile reasserts itself
instinct with a return
so outrageous and so shameless;
the smile the smile
always the same
            an uncaging
              a freedom.

Funland

1. The Superintendent

With considerable poise
the superintendent
has been sitting for hours now
at the polished table.

Outside the tall window
all manner of items
have been thundering down
boom boom stagily
the junk of heaven.

A harp with the nerves missing
the somewhat rusty
sheet-iron wings of an angel
a small bent tubular hoop
still flickering flickering
like fluorescent lighting
when first switched on
various other religious hardware
Elijah's burnt-out chariot
and to cap it all
you may not believe this
a red Edwardian pillar box.

My atheist uncle has been standing
in the corner wrathfully.
Fat Blondie in her pink
transparent nightdress
has been kneeling
on the brown linoleum.

And for some queer reason
our American guest yells
from time to time Mari-*an*
if they give you chewing gum
. . . . .CHEW.

Meanwhile the superintendent
a cautious man usually
inclined for instance
to smile in millimetres
has begun to take a great risk.

Calm as usual
masterful as usual
he is drawing the plans of the void
working out its classical proportions.

2. *Anybody here seen any Thracians?*

The tall handsome man
whom the superintendent
has nicknamed Pythagoras
asked fat Blondie
as she reclined strategically
under the cherry blossom
to join his Society.

The day after that
despite initial fleerings
my uncle also agreed.
The day following another hundred.

Two more weeks everyone
had signed on the dotted line.

There are very few rules.
Members promise to abstain
from swallowing beans. They promise
not to pick up what has fallen
never to stir a fire with an iron
never to eat the heart of animals
never to walk on motorways
never to look in a mirror
that hangs beside a light.
All of us are happy with the rules.

But Pythagoras is not happy.
He wanted to found
a Society not a Religion
and a Society he says
washing his hands with moonlight
in a silver bowl
has to be exclusive.
Therefore someone must be banned.
Who? Who? Tell us Pythagoras.
The Thracians yes the Thracians.

But there are no Thracians among us.
We look left and right wondering
who of us could be a secret Thracian
wondering
who of us would say
with the voice of insurrection

I love you
not in a bullet proof room
and not with his eyes closed.

Pythagoras also maintains
that Thracians have blue hair and red eyes.
Now all day we loiter near the gates
hoping to encounter someone of this
description
so that what is now a Religion
can triumphantly become a Society.

3. *The Summer Conference*

On grassy lawns
modern black-garbed priests
and scientists in long white coats
confer and dally.

Soon the superintendent will begin
his arcane disquisition
on the new bizarre secret weapon.
Meanwhile I – surprise surprise –
observe something rather remarkable
over there.

Nobody else sees it (near the thornbush)
the coffin rising out of the ground
the old smelly magician himself no less
rising out of the coffin.

He gathers about him his mothy purple
cloak.

Daft and drunk with spells
he smiles lopsidedly.
His feet munch on gravel.

He is coming he is coming here
(Hi bright-eyes! Hiya bright-eyes!)
he is waving that unconvincing
wand he bought in Woolworths.
He has dipped it in a luminous
low-grade oil pool.
Bored with his own act he shouts
KEEP OFF THE GRASS.
and
JEHOVAH ONE BAAL NIL

Then a lightning flash ha ha
a bit of a rumble of thunder.
Nothing much you understand.
Why should the agéd peacock
stretch his wings?

At once the scientists take off
the priests hurry up
into the sky. They zoom.
They free-wheel high over rooftops
playing guitars;
they perform exquisite
figures of 8

but the old mediocre reprobate
merely shrinks them
then returns to his smelly coffin.
Slowly winking he pulls down the lid
slowly the coffin sinks into the ground.
(Bye bright-eyes! Arrivederci bright-eyes!)

I wave. I blink.
The thunder has cleared
the summer afternoon is vacated.
As if a cannon had been fired
doves and crows
circle the abandoned green lawns.

4. *The Poetry Reading*

Coughing and echo of echoes.
A lofty resonant public place.
It is the assembly hall.
Wooden chairs on wooden planks.
Suddenly he enters suddenly
a hush but for the small
distraction of one chair
squeaking in torment on a plank
then his voice unnatural.

He is an underground vatic poet.
His purple plastic coat is enchanting.
Indeed he is chanting
Fu-er-uck Fu-er-uck
with spiritual concentration.

Most of us laugh
because the others are laughing
most of us clap
because the others are clapping.

In the Interval out of focus
in the foyer Mr Poet signs his books.
My atheist uncle asseverates
that opus you read Fuck Fuck—
a most affecting and effective
social protest Mr Poet.

In the ladies corner though
Marian eyeing the bard
maintains he is a real
sexual messiah
that his poem was not an expletive
but an incitement.
Fat Blondie cannot cease from crying.
She thinks his poem so nostalgic.

Meanwhile the superintendent asks
Mr Poet what is a poem?
The first words Eve spoke to Adam?
The last words Adam spoke to Eve
as they slouched from Paradise?

Mr Poet trembles
he whistles
he shakes his head Oi Oi.
As if his legs were under water

he lifts up and down in slow motion
up and down his heavy feet
he rubs the blood vessels in his eyes
he punches with a steady rhythm
his forehead
and then at last
there is the sound of gritty clockwork
the sound of a great whirring.

He is trying to say something.

His sputum is ostentatious
his voice comes through the long ago.

After the interval
the hall clatters raggedly into silence.
Somewhere else distant
a great black bell is beating
the sound of despair
and then is still.
Cu-er-unt Cu-er-unt chants the poet.
We applaud politely
wonder whether he is telling or asking.
The poet retires a trifle ill.
We can all see that he requires air.

5. *Visiting Day*

The superintendent told us
that last summer on vacation
he saw a blind poet

reading Homer
on a Greek mountainside.

As a result my atheist uncle
has fitted black lenses
into his spectacles.
They are so opaque
he cannot see through them.
He walks around with a white stick.
We shout Copycat Copycat.

In reply his mouth utters
I don't want to see I can't bear to see
any more junk dropping down.
Meanwhile visitors of different sizes
in circumspect clothes in small groups
are departing from the great lawns—
though one alone lags behind and is waving.

She in that blue orgone dress waving
reminds me how I wrote a letter once
'Love read this though it has little meaning
for by reading this you give me meaning'
I wrote or think I wrote or meant to write
and receiving no reply I heard
the silence.
Now I see a stranger waving.

October evenings are so moody.
A light has gone on
in the superintendent's office.

There are rumours that next week
all of us will be issued
with black specs.

Maybe yes maybe no.

But now the gates have closed
now under the huge unleafy trees
there is nobody.
Father father there is no-one.
We are only middle-aged.
There are too many ghosts already.
We remain behind like evergreens.

6. Autumn in Funland

These blue autumn days
we turn on the water taps.
Morse knockings in the pipes
dark pythagorean
interpretations.

The more we know
the more we journey into ignorance.

All day mysterious aeroplanes
fly over
leaving theurgic vapour trails
dishevelled by the wind
horizontal chalky lines
from some secret script

announcing names perhaps
of those about to die.

Downstairs the superintendent
sullen as a ruined millionaire
says nothing does nothing
stares through the dust-flecked window.
He will not dress a wound even.
He cannot stop a child from crying.

Again at night
shafting through the dark
on the bedroom walls
a veneer wash of radium
remarkably disguised
as simple moonlight.
My vertebral column
is turning into glass.

O remember
the atrocities of the Thracians.
They are deadly cunning.
Our water is polluted.
Our air is polluted.
Soon our orifices will bleed.

These black revolving nights
we are all funambulists.
The stars below us
the cerebellum disordered
we juggle on the edge of the earth

one foot on earth
one foot over the abyss.

7. Death of the Superintendent

With considerable poise
in a darkening room
the superintendent sat immobile
for hours at the polished table.
His heart had stopped in the silence
between two beats.

Down with the Thracians.
Down with the Thracians
who think God has blue hair and red eyes.
Down with the bastard Thracians
who somehow killed our superintendent.

Yesterday the morning of the funeral
as instructed by Pythagoras
all members on waking kept their eyes closed
all stared at the blackness
in the back of their eyelids
all heard far away five ancient sounds fading.

Today it's very cold.
Fat Blondie stands inconsolable
in the middle of the goldfish pool.
She will not budge.
The musky waters have amputated her feet.
Both her eyes are crying simultaneously.

She holds her shoes in her right hand
and cries and cries.

Meantime our American guest tries
the sophistry of a song.
The only happiness we know she sings
is the happiness that's gone
and Mr Poet moans like a cello
that's most itself when most melancholy.

To all of this
my atheist uncle responds magnificently.
In his funeral black specs
he will be our new leader.
Look how spitting on his hands first
he climbs the flagpole.
Wild at the very top he shouts
I AM IMMORTAL.

8. Lots of Snow

First the skies losing height
then snow raging and the revolution bungled.
Afterwards in the silence
between two snowfalls
we deferred to our leader.
We are but shrubs not tall cedars.

Let Pythagoras be
an example to all Thracian spies

my tyrant uncle cried
retiring to the blackness inside
a fat Edwardian pillar box.

Who's next for the icepick?

Already the severed head of Pythagoras
transforms the flagpole
into a singularly
long white neck.

It has become a god that cannot see
how the sun drips its dilutions
on dumpy snowacres.

And I? I write a letter to someone nameless
in white ink on white paper
to an address unknown.
Oh love I write
surely love was no less
because less uttered or more accepted?

My bowels are made of glass.
The western skies try to rouge the snow.
I goosestep across this junk of heaven
to post my blank envelope.

Slowly night begins in the corner
where two walls meet.
The cold is on the crocus.

Snows mush and melt
and small lights fall from twigs.

Bright argus-eyed the thornbush

Approaching the pillar box
I hear its slit of darkness screaming
griefless oaths and orders.

9. *The End of Funland*

Uncle stood behind me
when I read Mr Poet's poster
on the billiard cloth
of the noticeboard:
COME TO THE THORNBUSH TONIGHT
HEAR THE VOICES ENTANGLED IN IT
MERLIN'S
MESMER'S
ALL THE UNSTABLE MAGICIANS
YEH YEH
DR BOMBASTUS TOO
FULL SUPPORTING CAST.

Not me I said thank you no
I'm a rational man touch wood.
Mesmer is dead these many years
and his purple cloak in rags.

They are all dead replied uncle
don't you know yet
        all of them dead –

gone where they don't play billiards
haven't you heard the news?
And Elijah the meths drinker
what about Elijah I asked
who used to lie on a parkbench
in bearded sleep – he too?

Of course sneered uncle
smashed smashed years ago like the rest of them
gone with the ravens gone with the lightning.
Why else each springtime
with the opening of a door
no-one's there?

Now at the midnight ritual
we invoke Elijah Merlin Mesmer the best of them
gone with the ravens gone with the lightning
as we stand as usual in concentric circles
around the thornbush.
Something will happen tonight.

Next to me fat Blondie sobs.
Latterly she is much given to sobbing.
The more she sobs the more she suffers.

Suddenly above us
frightful insane
the full moon breaks free from a cloud
stares both ways
and the stars in their stalls tremble.

It enters the black arena aghast
at being seen and by what it can see.

It hoses cold fire over the crowd
over the snowacres of descending
unending slopes.

At last in the distance we hear
the transmigration of souls
like clarinets untranquil played by ghosts
that some fools think to be the wind.

Fat Blondie stops her crying
tilts her face towards me amazed
and holds my hand as if I too were dying.
For a moment I feel as clean as snow.

Do not be misled I say
sometimes Funland can be beautiful
But she takes her hand away.

I can see right through her.
She has become luminous glass.
She is dreaming of the abyss.
We are all dreaming of the abyss
when we forget what we are dreaming of.

But now this so-called moonlight
is changing us all to glass.
We must disperse say goodbye.
We cannot see each other.
Goodbye Blondie goodbye uncle goodbye

Footsteps in the snow
resume slowly up the slope.

They gave me chewing gum so I chewed.

Who's next for the icepick?

Tell me are we ice or are we glass?

Ask Abaris who stroked my gold thigh.

Fu-er-uck fu-er-uck.

Do not wake us. We may die.

Carnal Knowledge

1

You, student, whistling those elusive bits
of Schubert when phut, phut, phut, throbbed the sky
of London. Listen: the servo-engine cut
and the silence was not the desired silence
between two movements of music. Then
Finale, the Aldwych echo of crunch
and the urgent ambulances loaded
with the fresh dead. You, young, whistled again,
entered King's, climbed the stone-murky steps
to the high and brilliant Dissecting Room
where nameless others, naked on the slabs,
reclined in disgraceful silences – twenty
amazing sculptures waiting to be vandalized.

2

You, corpse, I pried into your bloodless meat
without the morbid curiosity of Vesalius,
did not care that the great Galen was wrong,
Avicenna mistaken, that they had described
the approximate structure of pigs and monkeys
rather than the human body. With scalpel
I dug deep into your stale formaldehyde
unaware of Pope Boniface's decree
but, as instructed, violated you –
the reek of you in my eyes, my nostrils,
clothes, in the kisses of my girlfriends.
You, anonymous. Who were you, mister?
Your thin mouth could not reply, 'Absent, sir,'
or utter with inquisitionary rage.

Your neck exposed, muscles, nerves, vessels,
a mere coloured plate in some anatomy book;
your right hand, too, dissected, never belonged,
it seemed, to somebody once shockingly alive,
never held, surely, another hand in greeting
or tenderness, never clenched a fist in anger,
never took up a pen to sign an authentic name.
You, dead man, Thing, each day, each week,
each month, you, slowly decreasing Thing,
visibly losing Divine proportions,
you residue, mere trunk of a man's body,
you, X, legless, armless, headless Thing
that I dissected so casually.
Then went downstairs to drink wartime coffee.

3

When the hospital priest, Father Jerome,
remarked, 'The Devil made the lower parts
of a man's body, God the upper,'
I said, 'Father, it's the other way round.'
So, the anatomy course over, Jerome,
thanatologist, did not invite me
to the Special Service for the Twenty Dead,
did not say to me, 'Come for the relatives' sake.'
(Surprise, surprise, that they had relatives,
those lifeless-size, innominate creatures.)

Other students accepted, joined in the fake chanting,
organ solemnity, cobwebbed theatre.
And that's all it would have been,

a ceremony propitious and routine,
an obligation forgotten soon enough
had not the strict priest with premeditated rage
called out the Register of the Twenty Dead –
each non-cephalic carcass gloatingly identified
with a local habitation and a name
till one by one, made culpable, the students cried.

4

I did not learn the name of my intimate,
the twentieth sculpture, the one next to the door.
No matter. Now all these years later
I know those twenty sculptures were but one,
the same one duplicated. You.
I hear not Father Jerome but St Jerome cry,
'No, John will be John, Mary will be Mary,'
as if the dead would have ears to hear
the Register on Judgement Day.
   Look, on gravestones many names.
There should be one only. Yours.
No, not even one since you have no name.
In the newspapers' memorial columns
many names. A joke.
On the canvases of masterpieces
the same figure always in disguise. Yours.
Even in the portraits of the old anchorite
fingering a dry skull you are half concealed
lest onlookers should turn away blinded.
In certain music, too, with its sound of loss,

in that Schubert Quintet, for instance,
you are there in the Adagio,
playing the third cello that cannot be heard.
   You are there and there and there, nameless,
and here I am, older by far and nearer,
perplexed, trying to recall what you looked like
before I dissected your face – you, threat,
molesting presence, and I in a white coat
your enemy, in a purple one, your nuncio,
writing this while a winter twig, not you,
scrapes, scrapes the windowpane.
   Soon I shall climb the stairs. Gratefully,
I shall wind up the usual clock at bedtime
(the steam vanishing from the bathroom mirror)
with my hand, my living hand.

Events Leading to the Conception of Solomon, the Wise Child

And David comforted Bathsheba his wife, and went into her, and lay with her; and she bore a son, and he called his name Solomon: and the Lord loved him

I

Are the omina favourable?
Scribes know the King's spittle,
even the most honoured
like Seraiah the Canaanite,
and there are those, addicted,
who inhale
          the smoke of burning papyrus.

So is the date-wine sour, the lemon sweet?
Who can hear the sun's furnace?

The shadow of some great bird
          drifts indolently
across the ochres and umbers
of the afternoon hills
          that surround Jerusalem.
Their rising contours, their heat-refracting
          undulations.

The lizard is on the ledges,
the snake is in the crevices.

It is where Time lives.

Below, within the thermals of the Royal
          City,
past the cursing camel driver,

past the sweating woman carrying water
            in a goatskin,
past the leper peeping through
            the lateral slats
of his fly-mongering latrine
to the walls of the Palace itself,
the chanting King is at prayer.

            Aha, aha,
attend to my cry, O Lord
who makest beauty
to be consumed away like a moth;
purge me with hyssop and I
            shall be clean.
Wash me and I shall be whiter
        than the blossom.
Blot out my iniquities.

Not yet this prayer, not yet
            that psalm.
It is where a story begins.
Even the bedouin beside their black tents
have heard the desert wind's rumour.
They ask:
            Can papyrus grow
where there is no marsh?
They cry:
            Sopher yodea
to the Scribe with two tongues,
urge him to tend his kingdom
of impertinence.

II

When the naked lady stooped to bathe
    in the gushings of a spring,
the voyeur on the tower roof
    just happened to be the King.

She was summoned to the Palace
    where the King displayed his charms;
he stroked the harp's glissandos,
    sang her a couple of psalms.

Majestic sweet-talk in the Palace
    – he name-dropped Goliath and Saul –
till only one candle-flame flickered
    and two shadows moved close on the wall.

Of course she hankered for the Palace.
    Royal charisma switched her on.
Her husband snored at the Eastern Front,
    so first a kiss, then scruples gone.

Some say, 'Sweet victim in the Palace,'
    some say, 'Poor lady in his bed.'
But Bathsheba's teeth like milk were white,
    and her mouth like wine was red.

David, at breakfast, bit an apple.
    She, playful, giggling, seized his crown,
then the apple-flesh as usual
    after the bite turned brown.

III

In the kitchen, the gregarious, hovering flies
where the servants breakfast.
A peacock struts
        in its irradiance,
and is ignored.

On the stone floor and on the shelves
the lovely shapes of utensils,
great clay pots, many jugs of wine
        many horns of oil,
the food-vessels and the feast-boards.

On the long table, butter of kine, thin loaves,
bowls of olives and griddle-cakes,
wattled baskets of summer fruit,
flasks of asses' milk and jars of honey.

What a tumult of tongues,
        the maids and the men,
the hewers of wood,
the drawers of water,
        the narrow-skulled
        and the wide-faced.
What a momentary freedom prospers,
        a detour from routine,
a substitute for mild insurrection.

They ask:
  In his arras-hung chamber

did the King smell of the sheepcote?
On the ivory bench, did he seat her
        on cushions?
Did she lie on the braided crimson couch,
beneath her head pillows of goat hair?

Who saw him undo her raiments?
Who overheard Uriah's wife,
Bathsheba of the small voice,
        cry out?
Was it a woman made love to
or the nocturnal moan
        of the turtle dove?
Will the priest, Nathan, awaken
who, even in his sleep, mutters
        Abomination?

Now she who is beautiful to look upon
leaves furtively by a back door.
She will become a public secret.
She wears fresh garments of blue and purple,
the topaz of Ethiopia beneath her apparel.
But a wind gossips in the palm trees,
the anaphora of the wind
        in the fir-trees of Senir,
        in the cedars of Lebanon,
        in the oaks of Bashan.
It flaps the tents where Uriah, the Hittite,
is encamped with Joab's army
on the Eastern open fields.

Does purity of lust last one night only?
In the breakfasting kitchen, the peacock screams.

IV

The wind blows and the page turns over.
  Soon the King was reading a note.
Oh such excruciating Hebrew:
  'I've one in the bin,' she wrote.

Since scandal's bad for royal business
  the King must not father the child;
so he called Uriah from the front,
  shook his hand like a voter. Smiled.

Uriah had scorned the wind's whisper,
  raised his eyebrows in disbelief.
Still, here was the King praising his valour,
  here was the King granting him leave.

In uniform rough as a cat's tongue
  the soldier artlessly said,
'Hard are the stones on the Eastern Front,
  but, Sire, harder at home is my bed.'

Though flagons and goat-meat were offered
  the Hittite refused to go home.
He lingered outside the Palace gates,
  big eyes as dark as the tomb.

Silk merchants came and departed,
  they turned from Uriah appalled –

for the soldier sobbed in the stony heat,
ignored his wife when she called;

sat down with his sacks, sat in the sun,
sat under stars and would not quit,
scowled at the King accusingly
till the King got fed up with it.

'Stubborn Uriah, what do you want?
Land? Gold? Speak and I'll comply.'
Then two vultures creaked overhead
to brighten the Hittite's eye.

'Death.' That's what he sought in the desert
near some nameless stony track.
And there two vultures ate the soldier
with a dagger in his back.

The widow was brought to the Palace,
a Queen for the King-size bed,
and oh their teeth like milk were white,
and their mouths like wine were red.

V

Should there be merriment at a funeral?
Stones of Jerusalem, where is your lament?
Should her face not have been leper-ashen?
Should she not have torn at her apparel
bayed at the moon?
Is first young love
always a malady?

When Uriah roared with the Captains of Joab,
the swearing garrisons,
the dust leaping behind the chariots,
the wagons, the wheels;
when his sword was unsheathed
amidst the uplifted trumpets
and the cacophony of donkeys;
when he was fierce as a close-up,
huge with shield and helmet;
when his face was smeared with vermilion,
did she think of him less
than a scarecrow in a field?

When she was more girl than woman
who built for her
a house of four pillars?
When his foot was sore
did she not dip it in oil?
When his fever seemed perilous
did she not boil the figs?

When the morning stars sang together,
face to face, they sang together.
At night when she shyly stooped
did he not boldly soar?

When, at midnight, the owl screeched
who comforted her?
When the unclothed satyr danced
in moonlight
who raised a handkerchief to her wide eyes?

When the archers practised
        in the green pastures
whose steady arm curled about her waist?

True love is not briefly displayed
like the noon glory of the fig marigold.

Return oh return
pigeons of memory to your homing land.

But the scent was only a guest
        in the orange tree.
The colours faded
        from the ardent flowers
not wishing to outstay their visit.

VI

The wind blows and the page turns over.
    To Bathsheba a babe was born.
Alas, the child would not feed by day,
    by night coughed like a thunderstorm.

'Let there be justice after sunset,'
    cried Nathan, the raging priest.
Once again he cursed the ailing child
    and the women's sobs increased.

So the skeletal baby sickened
    while the King by the cot-side prayed

and the insomniac mother stared
   at a crack in the wall afraid.

Nobody played the psaltery,
   nobody dared the gameboard.
The red heifer and doves were slaughtered.
   A bored soldier cleaned his stained sword.

Courtiers huddled in the courtyard,
   rampant their whisperings of malice.
The concubines strutted their blacks.
   The spider was in the Palace.

Soon a battery of doors in the Palace,
   soon a weird shout, 'The child is dead.'
Then Bathsheba's teeth like milk were white,
   and her eyes like wine were red.

Outside the theatre of the shrine
   David's penitent spirit soared
beyond the trapped stars. He wept. He danced
   the dance of death before the Lord.

That night the King climbed to her bedroom.
   Gently he coaxed the bereaved
and in their shared and naked suffering
   the wise child, love, was conceived.

CODA

Over the rocky dorsals of the hills
the pilgrim buses of April arrive,
one by one, into Jerusalem.

There was a jackal on the site
        of the Temple
before the Temple was built.

And stones. The stones only.

Are the omina favourable?
Will there be blood on the thorn bush?
Does smoke rising from the rubbish dump
        veer to the West or to the East?
So much daylight! So much dust!
This scribe is
        and is not
the Scribe who knew the King's spittle.

After the soldier alighted,
a black-bearded, invalid-faced man,
stern as Nathan, head covered,
followed by a fat woman, a tourist
wearing the same Phoenician purple
        as once Bathsheba did,
her jewelled wrist, for one moment,
a drizzle of electric.

But no bizarre crowned phantom
will sign the Register
        at the King David Hotel.

Like the lethargic darkness
of 3000 years ago,
once captive, cornered

within the narrow-windowed
Temple of Solomon,
everything has vanished into the light.

Except the stones. The stones only.

There is a bazaar-loud haggling
in the chiaroscuro
of the alleyways,
tongue-gossip in the gravel walks,
even in the oven of the Squares,
a discontinuous, secret weeping
of a husband or wife, belittled and betrayed
behind the shut door of an unrecorded house.
There is a kissing of the stones,
a kneeling on the stones,
psalmody and hymnody,
winged prayers swarming in the domed hives
of mosques, synagogues, churches,
ebullitions of harsh religion.

– For thou art my lamp, O Lord . . .
– In the name of God, Lord of the Worlds . . .
– Hear the voice of my supplications . . .
– And forgive us our trespasses . . .
– The Lord is my shepherd I shall not want . . .
– My fortress, my high tower, my deliverer . . .
– The Lord is my shepherd I shall not . . .
. . . my buckler, my hiding place . . .
– I am poured out like water . . .
– The Lord is my shepherd . . .
. . . and my bones are vexed . . .

– The Lord is . . .
          – Allah Akbar!
          – Sovereign of the Universe!
          – Our Father in Heaven!
          – Father of Mercies!
          – Shema Yisroael!

There is a tremendous hush in the hills
          above the hills
where the lizard is on the ledges,
where the snake is in the crevices,
after the shadow of an aeroplane
          has hurtled and leapt
below the hills and on to the hills
          that surround Jerusalem.

The Abandoned

Du, Nachbar Gott . . .
R.M. Rilke

. . . thy absence doth excel
All distance known
George Herbert

I

God, when you came to our house
we let you in. Hunted,
we gave you succour,
bandaged your hands,
bathed your feet.

Wanting water we gave you wine.
Wanting bread we gave you meat.

Sometimes, God, you should recall
we are your hiding-place.
Take away these hands
and you would fall.

Outside, the afflicted pass.
We only have to call.
They would open you
with crutch and glass.

Who else then could we betray
if not you, the nearest?
God, how you watch us
and shrink away.

2

Never have we known you so transparent.
You stand against the curtain and wear
its exact design. And if a window opens
(like a sign) then is it you
or the colours which are blown apart?
As in a station, sitting in a carriage,
we wonder which of the waiting trains depart.

God, you can't help your presence
any more than the glassy air that lies
between tree and skies. No need to pass
through wave-lengths human ears can't sense.

We never hear the front door close when you are leaving.
Sometimes we question if you are there at all.
No need to be so self-effacing,
quiet as language of the roses
or moss upon a wall.

We have to hold our breath to hear you breathing.

3

Dear God in the end you had to go.
Dismissing you, your absence made us sane.
We keep the bread and wine for show.

The white horse galloped across the snow,
melted, leaving no hoofmarks in the rain.
Dear God, in the end, you had to go.

The winds of war and derelictions blow,
howling across the radioactive plain.
We keep the bread and wine for show.

Sometimes what we do not know we know –
in Armageddon town they write your name
dear God. In the end you had to go.

Yet boarding the last ship out we'd sorrow
that grape is but grape and grain is grain.
We keep the bread and wine for show.

Will world be leased to vulture and the crow?
Small lights upon the shore begin to wane.
Dear God in the end you had to go,
we keep the bread and wine for show.

4

They say, truant, you've vanished, address unknown,
that those who trusted you don't do so now
and, like the bereaved, feel empty and alone.

No wonder the plaudits for you grow fainter:
the George Herbert-like poems; the holy
plagiarism of each landscape painter.

And the congregations fewer for the sting of prayer,
all the fawning words, all the honeyless hum –
all for you, neighbour Gott. And you not there.

Still we call the Register. You're not excused.
Disease? Here sir. *Famine?* Present sir. *War?*
They say you fashioned us so who's accused?

5

Last night, awakened, did we hear you call?
Memory, father of tears, who was that knocking?
That incautious noise. Was there someone knocking?
Someone we once knew when we were small?

God, you have so many disguises. Once, we
from our dark bedroom cots, in mild fear,
could see how across the walls and ceiling
shadows of light would appear and flee.

This morning an omen downstairs on the floor,
a fallen picture frame. No homecoming,
no shadow of a shadow returning to stay,
no slow opening of a creaking door.

And our thoughts blank as an angel's mirror
since you, it seems, have travelled the other way
farther than all distance known, and further.

1957, 2008